Babes in Boots

Babes in Boots

Terry Manley

First impression: 2006
© Terry Manley and Y Lolfa Cyf., 2006

This book is subject to copyright and may not be reproduced by any means except for review purposes without the prior written consent of the publishers

Dinas is an imprint of Y Lolfa

Cover design: Y Lolfa

ISBN: 0 86243 859 4

Printed on acid-free and partly recycled paper
and published and bound in Wales by
Y Lolfa Cyf., Talybont, Ceredigion SY24 5AP
e-mail ylolfa@ylolfa.com
website www.ylolfa.com

Chapter 1

In her own country she was a princess; at least, that's what the other men in the hospital ward had said, and, today, this tall, elegant and dark-skinned physiotherapist was coming to teach me to walk.

Not having walked properly, or even stood up straight for a few years, due to a spinal injury, I had dreamt of this day. When finally I stood up, the ground seemed far away. Then, with a rigid back, which had been held straight by various means for so long, I transferred the weight from my left to right leg, my feet felt like steel flippers. In spite of the fearful feeling that my back would snap, I felt excitement; I could walk, albeit with a helping hand.

This then led to more serious therapy, exercising parts of my body that I had nursed for so long, in fear of yet more pain. Also, I had looked, for many a long hour, through hospital windows at people simply coming and going, which spoke to me of real freedom. They were moving on their own feet, upright and unaided. This had seemed to be as unattainable for me as the yacht of the millionaire.

Now, like a song title of the blues singers, Sonny Terry and Brownie McGee, it was a matter of '*Walk On*'.

Twelve weeks later, I stood on the Welsh summit of Snowdon. Next, it was Tryfan, via the north ridge, coming around to finish on the eastern buttresses, rope and all. I did get the shakes in my leg, which is a thing that all newcomers to rock-climbing will recognise, but in spite of that and 1,500 feet of fresh air beneath my feet, I felt at home. Then, there was the joy of looking down at the Menai Straits, as if I was looking at a relief map, and then, to reflect on how I'd attained that view. This area became synonymous with that joy which I'd experienced there, and, in spite of the glitter and gloss of city and college life, I never lost that experience, it having been deeply embroidered, as it were, on my heart. My fellow students, with whom I shared digs, would be dragged out of bed on Sunday mornings, and regularly walked over fields and along muddy riverbanks. This was until they, too, began to experience 'the freedom of our feet'; or 'walking God's good earth and not this concrete stuff', as one elderly lady had once put it to me, pointing as she spoke, to the paved path outside her bungalow.

It was this natural desire inherent in us all, to share with others the good things that we learn that probably caused my walking path to take the direction it did.

Starting as we meant to go on, my wife and I spent our honeymoon in a small tent, in North Wales; camping, this, of course, being the gateway to higher walking. Then, as time and life progressed, nappy buckets became part of our equipment. Modern, disposable baby pants hadn't been invented yet. I always remember one lady climber looking on as I self-consciously rinsed out the nappies in ice-cold water, with snow on the tops of the mountains for added emphasis.

"I must admire you; we always leave ours at home," she said, referring to her children.

It was little statements like this along the way that caused my wife and me to reconsider what we were doing. We had been worried about what others would think of our dragging young children up mountains; but to leave them at home with others while we

A wonderful piece of equipment

followed our selfish pursuits seemed even worse than taking them with us, we concluded.

It was thus that a very pleasant chapter in our life began, with a wonderful piece of equipment called the Papoose baby-carrier. Although this was an extra item to carry, it leaves both your hands free to put into your pockets, which, apparently, is the only way to climb Tryfan, according to some foolhardy braggarts. The only problem is that your partner has to keep a vigilant eye on your infant, who, while being lovingly jogged off to sleep, has to have its head propped up. As time passes, the load increasingly reminds you of its existence, due to an apparent steady increase in weight. Then, just as it becomes too uncomfortable; "I want to walk, Daddy," is the welcome call, and a much appreciated rest ensues.

At three years of age, a child is full of energy, but lacks stamina, and so our walking style had to be carefully monitored to suit young legs. Then, came one added problem; we had to get out the nappy-bucket again, and we were grounded for a little while. Nonetheless, after a bit of soul searching, and a bigger, almost family-sized tent, we found ourselves camping with an infant of just four weeks. A couple of months later, we tried a North Wales climb again. On the steep bits, I had to have the older bundle on my back, and the wee one in a 'cocoon' carrier, which was held around my neck with a cord, and held steady against my chest. I wondered if I was quite sane. It was at this time that I got another profound comment.

"They've got to have it, have they?" asked a passing walker, on the lower slopes of Moel Siabod. This prompted me to think once again about whether I was being fair, and if I should retire to deck chairs and Spanish swimming pools. However, because we seemed to do everything together as a family, in some queer way, it seemed logical to our illogical minds to carry on as we were.

Once again the march of time produced changes: the baby became a toddler and the previous toddler became a fine walker. I still felt a bit worried that we were pushing them into a predetermined mould, but that always seems inevitable to some degree, with very young children, because they have to come with you, or be moulded by their baby sitter. Ruth always took pride in her foot-ware, and I clearly remember her first encounter with the foot-gauge. Walking out of the shop and right across Nottingham, to the car (the longest walk yet), she was all the while watching herself walk, constantly pointing and reciting the word 'shoes'. With similar pride, she donned her first pair of boots. We still have those boots and are reluctant to part with them, despite a few moves.

The buying of equipment always seems to be concomitant with all hobbies and interests. It can sometimes get out of hand and become an obsession in itself, or a status symbol, to the exclusion of other needs and pleasures. However, it was certainly true that Ruth was helped by a simple piece of equipment. She had seen many be-sacked walkers and climbers in her short life span, possession of a rucksack became the temporary dream to eat her heart away; that is, until a Bambino 1 (a fitting name) became her pride and joy, and, of course, she had to walk to flaunt her worldly goods. Subsequently, Ruth marched up to Llyn Bochllwyd, arguing that she could carry this, and that wasn't too heavy. The next time, when she was about four years of age, she went to the top of Tryfan and looked down in amazement, and thought, as I have often done, that it's difficult to relate what you see to reality, because it lies so far below. This angle on the world around us is what we find so difficult to accept, hence the dizzy-heights feeling experienced by many. However, after a truly beautiful day, we skipped home to dinner.

Many fine holidays followed this, and also many a stolen weekend was enjoyed, as well as the walking of local rights of way. We exercised these walking routes carefully, studying maps and always looking for circular routes back to the car, or to our house. Sometimes, we'd take lunch with us, or plan it so that lunch-time and pub opening-time would coincide, but often it was the village sweet shop that made our spirits soar, as we crossed stiles, discussing the merits of one chocolate or sweet against another. We usually agreed that the Callard and Bowser's packet range was the best, but there was further debate about which of them we fancied. Were we to have the barley sugar, or the treacle brittle? Then, to make matters even more gluttonous, the conversation would turn to the age-old question which haunts all wives and mothers, "What's for tea?" Often, tea had been left in the icebox, back at the car park. As we settled down to enjoy the food, we would watch the sun go down and see others going home to prepare their tea. On the drive home, we felt that we'd squeezed the last out of the day, or had we? The sack of dirty boots would be put in the shed, with solemn promises to clean them the next day.

After everyone had washed, we would sit round the fire with pop, home-made beer and crisps, to relive the day, and plan with greater enthusiasm the next expedition. If it had been a particularly gruelling day, we'd discuss easier routes, or even, dare I say it, trips to the zoo, or deck-chaired afternoons in the garden, and many of those we enjoyed, too.

As Ruth and Joanna grew, along with their feet, which seemed constantly to need new boots, so also our horizons grew a little. Without overdoing it and pushing them too far, we saw fresh things and reached new heights. However, I found myself having to hold back all the while, for fear that I'd put them off walking altogether. I always wanted them to see its joys, though I couldn't expect them to see it from quite the same point of view as myself, and so, sometimes, the trips would be short, but always day trips, even when we were on a long holiday. We would camp, and one day, we'd drive here, the next day, walk there, usually on a whim, our destination rarely planned.

It was on a trip such as this, that we walked, late one afternoon, up to Llyn Cowlyd in the Carneddau of North Wales. It had been a warm, calm day, and we sat on rocks near the lake's edge, eating biscuits, slicing apples, and commenting on how the very high rocks of Creigiau Gleison plunged into the water of this, then, very blue lake. This caused us to wonder how much more they plunged, before they reached the real bottom of the valley; and we discussed the collapse of the dam and the subsequent flooding of the village in the Conway valley below.

Then, something happened that was to have a profound effect on our walking life. A young couple walked by and said, "Hello," as all people who pursue the outdoor life seem to do, and then they walked on with their large rucksacks, which were crowned with bright yellow Karrimats. Their colourful image against the view we'd just been enjoying prompted, firstly, a photograph, then, a comment.

I asked, without thinking too much, "How would you like to be them? They don't know where they're going to spend the night.

The Carneddau mountain range is wild and covers a large area, and our couple's direction would not necessarily take them to any town or village by nightfall. It seemed romantic, it seemed exiting, and an idea was born. Back at the tent, I asked the question again, only this time, I was serious. Our walks were always limited; if we walked three miles in one direction, it was three miles to walk back. However, if we were backpacking, we could do six miles, and be taken into fresh territory.

In the weeks that followed, the logistics of turning my idea into reality was discussed. We had one smallish but heavy tent, one large rucksack, one day-sack, and the usual camping and walking equipment. We debated whether it would be wise to buy other equipment, when we might afterwards discover that we didn't like back-packing, and we finally decided that we would make do with and adapt what we already had. The papoose with a cover would serve as a rucksack, to carry heavier things, such as the tent, and the large rucksack could take the bulk of smaller things. With a new day-sack for Joanna, we'd have something to serve as a pack-a-back. The tent was another item we had to consider. With an extension on the groundsheet and flysheet, and the doors pegged out, we told ourselves that we could get two adults and two children and all the gear into a two-man tent. That was the theory, when we tried it out on the lawn at home. With the children's heads in the bell end and ours on the ground-sheet extension, and feet left to fight it out in the middle, it was going to be easy, we thought, without really thinking carefully about where to stow the kit. We'd find room for it somewhere, we said optimistically. As we'd be making our first assault in the summer, when the weather was bound to be good, we'd use our spare clothing in place of Karrimats. We had a Gaz-stove from earlier days, which worked fine in all but very cold weather, and so, it was now map-study time.

Anyone would think we were planning to undertake a Himalayan expedition, the way we studied maps for routes, and checked equipment, but it had to be a success, and it had to be accomplished with poor kit, as well; otherwise, the children would be put off altogether, and they were already showing signs of cooling-off. On one matter we had a hard and fast rule: that we had to be able to get back to the car within one day, should we have to give up due to bad weather, injury, sickness, or just being sick of walking. The walk also had to be adaptable to changes of plan made *en route*. Try as I would, I couldn't plan a walk that would work if we followed the direction taken by our Carneddau backpackers. We finally settled for a route that would take us around the back of Moel Siabod, through Tanygrisiau, and back to Capel Curig.

Chapter 2

The great day arrived. We'd decided to sleep in the small tent on the night before we set out, thereby starting off as we meant to carry on; also, it would be quicker to pack up in the morning. We had the big tent for when we came back to base. We slept well, in spite of being cramped. I stirred at about seven but we didn't get up till nine.

(It's worth taking note of the times as the days pass by.)

We awoke to typical Welsh weather: a deluge of rain. Taking down the tent made us feel all the more exposed to our own doubts about the wisdom of what we were about to do. We found ourselves trying to read each other's thoughts; each of us wondered whether we were still going. The farmer must have taken pity on us, because he said we should finish packing in the barn, where we also finished our breakfast, savouring this last contact with civilisation.

I talked to the farmer's older son about their winter sheep losses, and learnt that his family had been tenants for generations. This led him to tell me how he'd given up well paid engineering work abroad, and come back to hill farming, to work with his dad. This was with a view to claiming the tenancy of the farm, before it was turned into a proposed National Park camping-site. I thought this was quite something in the way of a sacrifice, when one considers that remote Welsh hill farms have disappeared rapidly in the last fifty years. The life, that seems so romantic to town and city dwellers, involves such hard, persistent work in bitter, long-lasting winters that it's inevitable that this lifestyle would die away.

We had recently spoken to an elderly couple, who lived on a smallholding in the Brecon Beacons National Park. As we sat by their fire, the draught was cutting us in pieces, and there was a block of ice in a bowl on the floor. This was their water supply for the day. The large, brass, coldwater tap was by the door; underneath it was a bowl, which was perched on a chair. The tap, however, was out of action. This, along with electricity, was their recent approach to modernization. We marvelled at how previous generations had survived in a place like this, 1,200 feet above sea-level and miles from a village, never mind a town. The wife told us how they intended to close the place next January and February, and go to stay with their son in Birmingham. Who would blame them?

This natural drift towards modern comforts leaves behind many a museum piece, to decay on Welsh and Scottish moors. Interestingly, the area where they lived is named Hafod, which is the Welsh word for a summer residence. Perhaps, the former generations of farmers here were wiser than we think, assuming from its name that the place was only inhabited during the warmer months of the year.

Our packing done, we left the farm and set off on our walk, passing a Tramp back-packing tent, which caused me enviously to bemoan the smallness of our vagabond tent. We also passed a camping comedian, who was talking to a young cyclist, and we heard him asking the cyclist how much he got to the gallon.

At 11.30am, we broke contact with our modern comforts, that is, with the exception of those few that we carried on our backs, and made good time on the way to Capel Curig. We stopped just before getting there, to enjoy a lunch of soup, bakestones and tea. We were near a large boulder, which seemed to offer the stove little protection from the wind, and the watched kettle struggled slowly to the boil. We eventually drank our tea, but it was already

2.30pm before we walked down into Capel Curig.

We have always loved to wander around this very mountainous village, just enjoying its atmosphere. After the toilet ritual, and shopping for bread, apples, pork pies and salad for tea, we dragged ourselves reluctantly away from this pampering village, and walked along the road to Pont Cyfyng. It was even more of a drag than the first stage had been, because I had to go back again, to look for Ruth's woolly hat. Fortunately, I found it before I had retraced my steps any distance. We walked up behind a little chapel, with the words of the author, Showell Styles, ringing in my ears: 'No uphill after three.' We weren't going to make it to our scheduled campsite that night, and so we camped rough, or wild, as some say, hoping that the landowner would forgive us.

We all experienced the relief of swinging our packs to the ground, in the knowledge that that was it for the day. You still feel the straps that aren't there any more, and also the light and springy feeling you experience, having shed the burden, makes you feel as if you're going to topple forward.

We suffered from a plague of flies during our tea. This was followed by a swarm of midges, then, at dusk, we saw, and I thought I even heard, bats. It was a clear, calm and cloudless evening, the mountains showing up in varying shades of blue. We were glad that we'd decided to come, and slept in a way that only those who work with their hands know how, although we had done it with our feet.

They say that things look better in the morning, and that was true for us, when we rose at 7.45am. We saw the mist rising off Moel Siabod, the dew on the ground, and heard blue tits in the trees below us. We felt at home in our snug canvas house, with its little cooker and fluffed up sleeping bag beds. After Ruth had got her socks wet, we hung them out on the gypsy-line, a nearby hedge, to dry in the weak, morning sunshine. This morning, we were away by 10.20am, feeling very pleased with ourselves. That is, until we passed a bull on the top. At first, we were only concerned with getting past him and away. Then, the penny dropped; we hadn't crossed a stile, a fence, or gone through a gate or hedge, since leaving our site for the night; and we had slept so peacefully. Certainly, our ignorance had been bliss, and I dreaded to think about what could have happened if our companion of the night had investigated us closely.

After passing a couple walking their dog, we came down into a large wood, which seemed eerily still and quiet. Then, as we stopped for lunch, we heard the shouts of children, and family parties walked silently past, observing, from the corner of their eyes, what must have appeared to them to be a very odd brood. Later, we stopped on a little bridge over a stream, which was still within the wood. It was getting hot and the air was still; a cloud of butterflies crowned the height of summer with their fleeting flashes of colour. They were mainly tortoiseshells, red admirals and peacocks, and to see them all at once, and in one place, was really something special.

We came out of the wood quite suddenly, and saw the village of Dolwyddelan in the valley below us. This was a valley that was new and fresh to us, affording a pleasant view of a pleasant place. The pasture seemed lush as we walked down into the village, where there were cars and people, with their usual noise and bustle. Nonetheless, the sight of displays of lagers, beers, fruit-drinks and lemonade caused us to overlook the hustle and bustle.

"Mind the rucksacks. What do you want?" I took their orders and went towards the public house.

"Sorry, sir, we're closed."

I looked at my watch and saw that it was ten minutes past closing time. I'd forgotten already how the modern world is governed by time. Not to be beaten, over the road we went, to a shop, and bought cans of shandy and ginger beer, and replenished our stock of fresh food. The children bought their usual summer flip-flops, and away down the road we went, in the direction of some little splashes of orange and blue. As we got nearer to them, we were thankful to see them materialized into a campsite. Walking along the noisy, tiring road, we saw a garden and a lady, spinning wool, on her cottage doorstep. In the afternoon sun, this scene spoke of a different age, far removed from the digital, plastic unreality of the present time.

As we walked onto the campsite, I joked about the tin-shacks in the corner, saying how funny it would be if they were the toilets. They were! Nonetheless, it was a very suitable place, because we could rest and relax in very pleasant surroundings, after another day full of good things. It was quiet, and, with a fast flowing stream for a washbasin, and its cleaner than tap water contents, it was five-star accommodation. We had, by now, dropped way behind on our schedule, and were doing a shorter circuit of Moel Siabod; but we were on holiday. Therefore, we celebrated the holiday, and had stewed steak, mixed vegetables and rice, followed by bananas and custard. Then, sitting back in the fresh air, we soaked up sunshine, tea and clear views. However, all good things come to an end, and it was probably the midges, as well as tired limbs, that caused us to be in bed by 9.15pm.

The morning greeted us with very heavy dew again, and Ruth and Joanna ran about, making green footprints in the grass. Due to the change of schedule, we now had a gas problem. The cartridge-piercing needle on the stove was, as I thought then, jammed down, because, when the new cartridge was screwed home, a lot of gas was wasted. We were unlikely to encounter any shops in the next couple of days, and I was worried about having enough gas to last us.

We left our kit behind and walked back into the village of Dolwyddelan. However, the post-office, which advertised gas for sale, was closed until after lunch. So, back we went and packed up our belongings. We went next to the farmhouse, not to pay the fee for our camping spot, which we'd done the day before, but we went to ask for the key of the castle. Just behind the farmhouse stands a majestic, square tower, not the remains of yet another Norman castle, but a real Welsh-built castle. It is here that the famous Welsh prince, Owen Glyndwr, was born, and it's difficult to get more Welsh than that. We scaled the ramparts and had lunch in the grounds, which were little more than a grass bank. Then, while the others waited on a nearby hill, I walked back a second time to the village.

In spite of the many adverts to the contrary, they didn't have any gas cartridges in the post-office. By now, I'd already walked a fair way, and yet had got nowhere. Therefore, it was a late start again. However, apart from this little niggling worry about gas, we were enjoying ourselves. Feeling very much at ease, we thought that the ordinary things in life seemed a long way off. I always find that it feels good when everyday matters take second place in life, and I also remember an advertisement, where a sophisticated voice says "Anyone who talks about cars, babies, or washing machines, never gets invited here again". It seemed so amusing, and yet, its thought-provoking truth gives it real weight.

Suddenly, as we went down a lane leading into a farmyard, we spotted an adder. There he had lain in peaceful solitude, until we disturbed him, when, suddenly, with amazing speed and agility, he slid away into one of the cracks of the wall that had been his sun-bed. We all seemed to point simultaneously, with open mouths and delayed reaction, then, in unison, exclaimed, "Look!" We talked of little else for some time, until the incline onto the moor became steeper; it was the first real uphill, and it was already past three in the afternoon. Now there came the inevitable, plaintive cry;

"How much farther? Where are we going to camp?"

Well, how would you say, "I don't know," and still sound knowledgeable?

I'd picked out a line, following the lower contours, and then found, at odd intervals, marker sticks with red stripes, similar to those found in remote passes in the Alps. These led us to a beautiful double or figure-of-eight-shaped lake. It had been very windy, and we pitched our tent within the shelter of a small, derelict building, and made ourselves comfortable, and enjoyed a tea of salad and garibaldi biscuits. Whilst in the tent, we hadn't noticed the wind dropping, and the development of an almost magical evening. We stepped outside and all was arrestingly calm and still, the silence broken only by the fish as they plopped, and rippled the still lake's surface. Even the midges seemed to be at peace with us, and didn't bite. I dipped my face in the lake, to wash, almost afraid to disturb its smooth, silken surface, only to find that it was soothingly warm. In spite of the wind, the sun had left its mark in more ways than one. I looked up, to see little spirals of mist rising from the lake's surface. They were like little coils or springs about eight or nine inches tall. Then, a faint wisp of a breeze blew, so that they all slid unbroken across the surface, just as though they were skating across ice. I had never heard of, and certainly never seen, anything like it before.

We had arrived at seven and were in bed at nine; it hardly

seemed possible that so many things had happened in the past two hours. Apart from Joanna getting poked in the eye with a bulrush, the day had turned out perfect.

The next day dawned fresh and new. Just as the grass and leaves seem greener every spring, a dawn in the mountains always seems fresher than the one before, its newness bright like a newly minted coin.

We found that our bed for the night had been on the rubble of the old building, but, with ones hip in a suitable hole, it was surprisingly comfortable. We had been up by 7.30am, and had watched the clear, morning sun creep down Clogwyn Bwlch Y Maen, pushing its dawn shadow away. The clouds that lightly blew over Yr Arddu enveloped us during breakfast but they soon cleared away. We saw three climbers on the skyline to the north of us, which was the nearest we had come to other people since leaving the castle, yesterday lunchtime. While we were packing up and drying things on the ruin wall, because once again the dew had been heavy, Ruth and Joanna enjoyed throwing stones into the lake. Then, of course, dad had to go and show off with his dam-buster skims over the surface. This was our boisterous farewell to this secluded or sequestered place, as the author, W. Poucher, might have called it.

We set off at 10.00am, going around the north side of the lake and climbing steadily. We watched some fighter-planes doing aerobatics overhead, but they only reminded us of the world we'd left behind, or seemed to have left behind, at least, which was something about which we had no desire to think for the time being.

Back at base, at the foot of Clogwyn Bwlch Y Maen, we climbed slowly up to the *bwlch* or gap. Joanna has always claimed that the energy tablets we ate half way up had helped her to do it. However, we weren't really expecting, or ready for, what lay in front of us at the top. A true vista of sheer beauty lay between us and Yr Wyddfa, or Snowdon itself. Just the faint crown of cloud at the summit, which always seems to be there, reminded us of its majestic height. It was here that we had lunch and thought how marvellous it was, to be at this place on this day and with the weather so good. I can well imagine that, in foul conditions, it could be a very lonely spot, and no place to linger. Today, we could relax and enjoy our lunch of crisp-bread with cheese or jam, followed by bake-stones, or welsh cakes, and garibaldi biscuits. There was nothing to drink, until we found a stream lower down, where, much to the delight of the children, I fell down, after sliding on the smooth grass slope. There was no proper path here, and we floundered around amid great tufts of grass and bog, but we finally crossed a large stream and mounted the roadway, just to the east of the famous Pen-y-Gwryd hotel.

The next planned section was to be over towards the Glyder range, camping somewhere suitable along the way, but the children had heard that buses passed this way and, with their aid, we could be back at the farm that very same day. With the gas situation as it was, I consented to their request. We subsequently stood in the disorderly queue, which straggled all over the grass verge outside the Pen-y-Gwryd hotel. The 1953 Everest team had trained in this area, and their signatures were put on the ceiling of one of the bars, before they left for Nepal.

If ever you think that bus fares are expensive, try walking for a few days first. It's hard to accept the fact that your forward movement is due to no effort on your part, and that the miles are just flying under your feet. I can still remember vividly, seeing Ruth and Joanna sitting in front of us, with the warm summer breeze blowing through the bus. Joanna turned round to us, with a smug grin of deep satisfaction all across her face, and her pack on her lap, not her back.

We'd only been away from Capel Curig for a few days, but it felt as if it were longer. It's strangely and consistently true, that, after just a few days in the mountains, it feels as if you've been away for a week or more. We bought some fresh meat and bread, and shared a large bottle of dandelion and burdock pop, before setting off back to the farm. When we were putting up the large tent, at five o'clock, it felt as if we were coming home. Then, we were able to enjoy such luxuries as second cups of tea. The meal was a simple rice stew, which was eaten in silence, a sure sign of a successful meal. The airbed was sheer bliss. Now we could nurse those tender hip bones.

The next few days were spent doing things which normal people do while on holiday, such as sightseeing, shopping and getting bored. The cure, we decided, would be a walk up Snowdon. We went via the Pyg Track, which, apart from the horseshoe path, is probably the most satisfying way to scale this majestic mound. We had lunch at Bwlch-y-Moch, which means gap or pass of the pig, which some think has something to do with Pyg Track, although the Welsh spelling does create some doubt. The path there takes you down into the basin of the Snowdon's circuit, with fine views of Llyn Llydaw below us, and, later, the dramatically picturesque Glaslyn, where the legendary sword Excalibur is supposed to have been discovered by King Arthur. It was now, as we passed other walkers, that we realized how fit we had become in just a few days, and it was almost embarrassing to see the children skipping past panting and puffing young men in their prime. It could be said that the hand brake was off; we had no rucksacks. The view from Snowdon is always breathtaking, but the fact became really obvious to us just then; the world was at our feet. We were hooked, and pronounced backpacking to be the best way to walk and to experience this life more fully.

The world was at our feet

Chapter 3

Our next question was: where do we go from here? Of course, with our newly found confidence, our first inclination was to consider ridiculously ambitious, long distance paths, such as the Pennine Way. At our rate of walking, these routes would take a month or more and not many people can get that amount of holiday at any one time of the year, and I had to find alternatives.

While I worked out mountain back-packing trips to suit our speed of walking, I noticed that the girls were getting a bit worried about where their Dad was going to take them. When would they be going to the seaside? Would all our holidays now be sacrificed on the altar of this new, mad craze of mountain worship?

Then, quite suddenly, the answer came clearly; it was possible to combine our walks with the seaside. Why should we not walk along the cliff tops at the seaside? The Pembrokeshire coastal path would be ideal, except that its length, which is nearly 200 miles, was too much for us to manage. A short stretch of coast, however, would do us nicely, especially a peninsula of about thirty miles, or there about. One might ask why we thought of a peninsula. The answer might seem obvious: we would finish quite close to where we'd started, and the car would always be within easy reach. The next question was, why not a peninsula in Pembrokeshire?

To cut a long story short and spare you the details, the Marloes-Dale peninsula became our dream for the next few months. Some extra equipment was bought, to make things a little more comfortable. We again found ourselves packing up in the rain, after showers during the night, sorting out this and that and what to leave behind in the car, and who's going to carry what and when. After much discussion about whether every item was really necessary and who was to carry it, the decisions were made, tapes tied and all that remained to be done was to arrange the car parking with the farmer, who, we were told, was at church and wouldn't be back until midday. You may be interested to know that we were camped at Howelston, near Little Haven.

The rain had stopped and we were pulling at the leash, anxious to be on our way. It appeared likely to be lunchtime before we could get started, and this is not the ideal time to start. However, we set off at 12.30pm, and stopped soon afterwards, to have lunch. Despite the negative side of things, the delay and the early rain, we had already seen the beauty of this coastline. It is unspoilt, so much so that it is repeatedly used for making films with an historical setting, because there are so few modern things in sight, very often, not even a fence or hedge.

Some people passed us and briefly stopped to speak to us as we ate our lunch, I thought I sensed their respect, and realized that they actually viewed us as experienced walkers. The elation was intoxicating. We were, at this time, indeed, experienced walkers

We marched off with revitalized vigour. We also mused, as we trotted along, on the fact that, every time we ate, we lightened our load. It's nice to have an incentive to eat and not to slim. We thought we saw a seal. Then, there were speedboats, churning their way through the peaceful and now sunny afternoon. We next watched fishermen tending their lobster pots, in a more modest craft, made more visible by their orange coats and floats. Along this section to Mill Haven, there's an unusual wooded section, where you experience the almost paradisiacal view through trees to the blue sea below. It was here that we saw our first little lizard, sitting, almost impossible to spot, on a log. We marvelled at his camouflage. At 3.45pm we came to our first bay and beach, at Mill Haven. The tide was in, but ebbing, which was perfect, in this area, where nearly all the beaches are covered at high tide. For the children, this was the seaside, except that they thought the seaweed made it a bit untidy and smelly, but in the fervour of shell collecting it was soon forgotten. Then it was boots off and into the sea for a paddle.

I had real problems now: I knew of no campsite within a few miles, it was getting late in the day. Worst of all, the girls wouldn't take too kindly to having to start off again, so near to tea-time, and while the sun shone on such a nice little beach. We decided to have tea, then, in the evening, put up the tent and hope to be away early in the morning. Tea consisted of our old standby: rice, Soya mince and dried mixed vegetables. This was followed by a good helping of dried apple flakes and instant custard, and then, finally, tea. There were still a few walkers about at 8.30.

As the daylight turned into twilight, Joanna spotted our first lighthouse, then, the tanker that was anchored not far out became a fairy light wonder. Birds sang, even after we were in bed. However, all was not as tranquil as we would have liked. Joanna was just getting over a cold, which is why cough-mixture got spilled over our sleeping bags in an overcrowded tent. Then, just to enliven things a bit more, I began to experience the symptoms of a developing cold. We even talked of fetching the car, so that it would be nearer for the last leg of the walk.

It rained during the night, but we awoke to a fine Monday morning and the last week in June. The ship we had seen the night before was a strange sight; it seemed to be swinging on its anchor and puffing smoke in all directions, but not really moving anywhere.

We set off at eleven and got to the little inlet of St Bride's itself just after midday. We seemed to be in a hurry to get through, which I have since regretted, because it was a strangely pleasant place. The hurry was due in part to Joanna and her fear of the skin-divers that were there at the time, I don't think she was completely convinced that they were human. A little farther, on at Tower Point, we had our lunch. It was one o'clock, which meant that our pace was slower than we had intended it to be.

It was here that a girl passed us as we sat munching. Later, we passed her as she sat at the top of Musselwick Sands. Here, we left the path, to go shopping in the village of Marloes, where we met the girl again. It turned out that she lived not far from us, in Leicestershire, and was waiting to go over to Skomer, to work as a temporary warden on the island of puffins and Manx-shearwaters. I believe that, in the world of ornithology, it was quite a privilege for her. She spoke with a lot of enthusiasm, but, for such a young person, she also spoke with much appreciation and knowledge. She told us about her recent sighting of a peregrine falcon. Then, getting out the map, she eagerly showed us the exact location. Her knowledge, how far she'd walked, and the fact that she was a girl, knocked a hole in my elation of yesterday at our own achievements. We admired her and wished there were more young people like her. It also brought out Judith's repeated wish that she had known about boots and rucksacks, at a younger age.

Marloes is a quiet little village with a small clock tower, which looks somewhat out of place. Nonetheless, it proudly stands, dedicated to William, Duke of Kensington. There's also a fine village pump, a sober reminder of the problem of how to acquire water when walking the coastline, as opposed to the mountains, with their many clear, fast-flowing streams. Ruth and Joanna bought some sun visors, while we posted cards and stocked up on provisions. Afterwards, we drank ginger beer and Coke. On the way back to our room for the night, at East Hook farm, we could still see the tanker broadside. She had been there all day, causing us to reflect on Milford Haven, which was not too far away now, although we wouldn't actually get there on this trip. We also saw some friendly jet fighters, but, more interestingly, we saw some furry caterpillars, blue butterflies and many and varied wild flowers. These gave us pleasant thoughts and feelings, and it caused us to think about the peacefulness of creation, even when the wind blows and the sea roars.

Tea comprised cold meat and tomatoes, with bread and cheese spread. When this simple fare is laid out on the grass, in hot sunshine, after a good day's walk, it becomes a regular banquet. We continued to talk about the day, and the many things we'd seen and heard. We wanted to recall them all, for fear they would fade away in our minds, due to their profusion and our imperfect memories. One image that struck me was the sight of the potato pickers, emptying the fields, the harvesting done, and yet it was still only June. This shows how mild the climate can be in this area. Before going to bed at half past nine, we looked yet again at the tanker. This time, it was lit up, and fast becoming our ship, along with our lighthouse.

Another beautiful day, and a full one at that, dawned for us at half past seven, which proved to be just the best time to see the tanker desert us, which happened at eight o'clock, and after all we'd said about it. We were away for quarter to ten, and half an hour of easy walking found us at Martin's Haven, feeling very pleased with ourselves. We came into the haven just as the boat was leaving for Skomer, and we strained our eyes, looking for our young ornithologist friend. Boats for Skomer leave here every day in the summer, but the nearby island of Skockholm was only open to private parties at that time. Here on the mainland, we walked around the Deer Park, where, incidentally, there are no deer. From this good vantage point we were able to see the strong current rage in between Skomer and the mainland. We also looked back along the length of coast we had walked, and had a job to believe that our modest walking had brought us so far. While we were having lunch above Deadman's Bay, our imaginations went a bit wild, thinking about how it was so named, but, with the sun shining on Skockholm Island, the area didn't give the appearance of the dangerous coast that it really is. Walking coast paths anywhere can present a number of surprises, due to the constant and sometimes dramatic changes in the scenery. However, we weren't really ready for the surprise of seeing Marloes Sands in full sun and surf. After we had gazed in awe for a while, we eagerly pressed on, to be in the sea before the tide closed the beach for the afternoon.

The surf seemed as good here as it is in North Cornwall, and we had to be constantly on the retreat from the incoming waves. At one point, caught in surf, foam and flurry, Judith half fell in, causing her watch to stop, although time did not. We filled our water bottles from a stream, and set off for Dale. The ups and downs were, as they always are, hard going. You gain height, only to lose it almost straight away. One particularly painful section, that day, was near a spot marked Hookses on the map, but all the effort and exhaustion was forgotten, when we saw the blue waters of West Dale Bay.

We decided to omit the actual Dale peninsula for the time being, and camp the night in Dale, assuming that there was a site in Dale. It was here also where we had the now strange experience of going away from the coast path, to come to the sea again. It was as if we had walked only about a mile inland, only to find ourselves back beside the sea, due to the peninsula being so narrow at this point.

We stopped at a house along the way, to buy some fresh lettuce, and were told that there would be no camping in Dale, but that there was a site about a mile or so outside the village. The mile proved to be a bit of a country mile, and on a hard road. The children found it really hard going, and I had to carry their rucksacks as well as nurse them along. Ruth struggled on, shrugging back the tears. Up till now, this was our longest and hardest day. Our reward was truly amazing. Little notices led us around a corner and into the front yard of a farm. There stood a wooden hut, with emblazoned upon it in large letters, the word OASIS.

"Come on in, my dears," said a kindly voice from the back room.

Really hard going

Ruth's favourite meal, at the time, was baked beans on toast, and that is what we had. I found it hard to believe how this place had seemingly appeared from nowhere. It wasn't a mirage, but a real oasis, and we all wallowed in the comfort of being sat at a table, with knives and forks. We enjoyed welsh cakes and chocolate biscuits, and a pot of tea, drunk from real teacups, followed by yet another pot of tea. Ruth's smiling face was the final reward. It was also reassuring to know that we had our bed for the night. The normal camping field was full, and so we had to pitch our tent at the back of the farm, in another field. It was all very nice, but we missed the sea. It was almost unnerving to be without it. We talked of the powerful scenery of the Deer Park, and the surf at Marloes. Then, feeling exhausted, we were all soon asleep, in spite of being near a road, and we had the compensation of hearing a curlew's call in the nearby estuary, just to remind us that the sea wasn't very far away.

The fact that the next day was Wednesday was of little consequence, and we awoke at seven, to what was to be a really flaming June day. After paying the camp fees, and our respects to the family's pet lamb, we set off in burning hot sunshine, to make our way back to Howelston. There was still the Dale peninsula to walk, but we'd decided to make that a day-walk, in view of the fact that the end and the beginning are less than a mile apart and also that its distance of seven miles is just right for a pleasant day's walk, especially as we would be minus our rucksacks. Once again, it was like home from home in the large tent, with all the attendant luxuries peculiar to this generation. We sprawled languidly on the grass, drank cans of beer, and caught up on the news by listening to the radio. Across the grass wafted the gastronomic titillation of someone's barbecue. In fact, over the next few days, the owners of the barbecue, a couple, came under our close scrutiny, the strong human instinct of being nosey being our excuse. They seemed to cook every meal on their little barbecue, even the bacon for breakfast. It nearly drove us crazy; we had to have one, and so we joined the then fashionable throngs flocking to go-ahead garages and warehouses that sported this newly found way to absolute living.

After a rest day, plus shower and laundry day, although it usually ends up being called Ice Cream day, we started to walk the Dale peninsula. This time, we would be walking clockwise, from Dale village to West Dale Bay. It was a pleasant day, made all the more so by our having no packs to carry, or the worry of where we would lay our heads that night. It was good to be sitting on the cliff tops again, eating lunch; however, today was made that extra special because we'd been able to carry more exotic food and drink. The Irish ferry coming out of Milford Haven prompted thoughts of those holidaymakers on board, who, for that brief moment, shared virtually the same spot as us, and yet we were in different worlds.

The next bay is a little gem, and discerning people, who had walked there, carrying their beach paraphernalia, became the subjects of our envied attention as we walked high above them, and proceed to the next little cove. Here lay the twisted remains of a shipwreck, making the lighthouse beyond at St Anne's Head seem more than just a tourist attraction, as indeed it was for us that day.

When we went to investigate it closely, the officer in charge reeled off his informative patter, as he had obviously done many times before. However, the place smacked of efficiency and predictability, everything firm and clean, like the walls that support the electric filament, which is so thin and yet so powerful. It is also reliably efficient, due in part to its being changed regularly, after a period of use. We looked in awe at the almost magical glasswork, so intricate and sculptural, and yet it is no product of aesthetic art. The thing that has since stuck in our minds, and has been the theme of many conversations, was his explanation of the red sector, the purpose of which is to warn ships that they are within the firing range of the artillery based at Castlemartin. This was another grim reminder of the unpredictable, corrupt and polluted world in which we live, and yet, that all seemed to be on the other side of the water, on this particular day.

Turning back down the other side of St Anne's Head, the spectacular folds and subsequent deposit of rocks took us back in history, not only geologically, but also nautically, to the treachery of this coast to ships without modern navigational aids. Though a peaceful place to us, we could well imagine its unmerciful savagery, when ravaged by gale and tempest and the darkness of night. We dropped down to West Dale Bay, approaching, this time, from the opposite side, a little saddened to think that our little expedition, with all its long planning and preparation, was over. I took the last photograph of an anti-climaxed party, and posted the film in Dale, hoping that the slides would be on our doormat by the next weekend. This would enable us to recall some of the many things we had seen, heard, smelt, and even tasted, in our marathon holiday of one week. We had certainly all enjoyed it very much, and we vowed to return for another helping, later that summer.

Chapter 4

We were fortunate to have a comprehensive range of Ordinance Survey maps in our local library, which made it possible for us to study all the various possibilities for our next walk. When the choice had been made, we would buy only the map or maps needed.

It happened that the next planned walk kept us on the same map as before, when we intended to walk from Newgale to Porth Mawr, or Whitesands Bay. This would be a departure from our usual circular tour, but a main road runs parallel with the coastline, and, once again, we would savour the delights of a bus ride, after a few days walking. This stretch was also chosen because it appeared to have plenty of campsites, and this was an attractive feature, following our little episodes in June. The evening when we arrived was beautiful, one of those where the humid evening of a damp day is lightened by the sun's appearance just before sunset. Just when you think that it's all over, a glorious panorama of colour spreads across the underside of the clouds, turning the whole sky into the colour of a fiery furnace. While being a great marvel in itself, it also suggested that we could be fortunate with the weather. Being up at 7.30, and packed in three hours was a reflection of our enthusiasm the next day. We made arrangements to park the car, and called in at one of Newgale's shops, which, for such a small place, are excellent and obviously cater for a relatively fashionable clientele.

After a short climb, steep at first, and then easing off onto the cliff tops, our life since June seemed to have been but a short interlude.

Here we were, back again among the butterflies, furry caterpillars, grasshoppers and the greenery; and to crown it all was the sunshine. It sparkled on the blue sea; it reflected the chrome yellow of gorse, and the rainbow colours of the grasses, and purple heathers, which were now in full flower.

We passed a couple, who commented on the magnificent views, as if the magic of the moment was in the air, and we shared the moment together telepathically. We came close to a family sunbathing, and so early, outside their holiday cottage, and realized that we didn't envy them too much on this occasion, as the view from what might be called our veranda was constantly changing. When it changed to a little grassy dell with its gurgling stream, we decided to sit there and eat our lunch of fresh bread and pâté, followed by fresh fruit, biscuits and bakestones, washed down with fresh blackcurrant juice. You could call it a reFRESHing meal.

The stream could just be heard above the sound of the surf, and it led down to a very small beach, on which a family played. They had left their yacht bobbing about just offshore, while they enjoyed their private retreat. However, every one of us was enjoying the glory of creation, along with life itself, each in our own particular way.

Solva is, understandably, a popular place, but coming into it along the coast path is rather a long drawn out experience, due to the shape of the estuary. Initially, you find yourself going up and down a few times, and then, you have to go inland a good way, to come to Solva village. One has to go back out in a seaward direction, almost as if one has to pay for the rewards of being in the village, with its many attractions. The big attraction for us that day was a plentiful supply of canned drinks and ice cream. There was a lot to stand in front of, and stare at, but, after quite a long, hot day, we wanted to see what Mutton Farm looked like, especially with full stomachs, and our beds rolled out, waiting to nurse our weary bodies.

It turned out to be a homely place, complete with a palm tree. This was another reminder of the mild climate in the area. Joanna was greatly amused at two lads from the farm, who had an old Moped. They repeatedly raced around part of the field, which had a big dip in it, to suit their purpose. Watching them and their antics produced uncontrollable giggles from our Joanna. We also watched some trainee pilots from the nearby airfield, doing twists and loops, all free entertainment following our evening meal. There was also an interesting incident that took place when I went to pay the camp fees. I had started to fill in the visitors' book and had put my two pounds fee on the kitchen table, when I came to the column marked Car Registration Number. I looked up at the farmer, ready to explain that my car was at Newgale, and to ask whether I should put down the number.

"Oh, forget about that," he said, grabbing the book. "Just give us a pound."

Reduced rate for walkers! Like a kid with a lollipop, I couldn't wait to get back to tell the others. We then had a bit of mad half hour, trying to have showers in an unlit shower block, as the light faded, and the feathery clouds of sunset led into a starry night, so clear and still that the flashes of a lighthouse could be plainly seen the other side of the adjacent road. I've still not worked out for sure which lighthouse it was. Its four flashes reminded us that not everyone was at home that night.

Although we were awake at 7.30, the fact that it had clouded over may have accounted for the 8.30 rise, but it was to be a short stretch today, on the brambly way to Caerfai Bay. It was during this day that we actually saw two other backpackers; one was a man walking alone, and the other was a girl with a dog. We subsequently discussed at some length what would happen to the dog at night. We also saw our only vehicle on the coast-path, a Land Rover, the driver of which was not going all the way; he was just attending to some animals. A little way before we came to Caerfai, a woman with two dogs saw us taking photographs. She kindly offered to take a picture of us, with our camera, which I considered was a very thoughtful gesture. As most families will know only too well, photographically speaking, you're usually one member short, and it's frustratingly difficult to explain to a very young child that someone had to take the photograph and couldn't be in the picture as well. After getting to our next farm, at one o'clock, we found that the rate here was seventy pence per person, which meant that, strictly speaking it should have been two pounds and eighty pence for the four of us, but, once again, we learnt that the rate was reduced to fifty pence each for walkers, and the girls were classed as one. This appealed to my Scrooge-like streak because it worked out at nearly half price. We spent the afternoon on the beach, and went shopping in St David's later on, where we purchased fresh salad for our tea, along with cans of lager and pop. We were able to see a ship anchored in the centre of St Brides Bay, and that reminded us of the good times in June.

We then started to pick out places that were now familiar, on the other side of the bay. We also saw two lighthouses besides our four-flasher, as we went up to use the very meagre flow of hot water from the shower, to wash ourselves and our clothes; it wouldn't work as a shower. We also made a mental note that the site would be closed after September the sixth, and that it was now the first of that month.

The next day, Tuesday, was misty. It found us awake at seven and up by seven forty-five. Part way through breakfast, a woman on the site kindly offered us some hot water she had left over. Whether she'd taken pity on us I don't know, but it would save some of our gas, although we had restocked on the previous day. The sudden appearance of a low-flying jet was taken as a forecast of fine weather, when we set off at ten o'clock. At eleven o'clock we were at Porthclais, where there is a small harbour and not much more. It is reported that St Patrick sailed from here, when he voyaged to Ireland, to convert the native population. People greeted us as we passed along the path, but the fishing-lads at Pothclais were different, and not wishing to misjudge them, we decided that they were so engrossed in their work that they were oblivious to all else. One can see where the old breakwater has been repaired in recent years, to accommodate recreational yachtsmen. The line of limekilns along the side of the harbour had also been repaired. I must say that it had been very tastefully done, thus giving the area a park-like quality. We stared almost in disbelief at the notice over what served as his office door, proclaiming this to be the Harbour Master's office. The notice was screwed to a small garden shed. It was as unexpected as it was incongruous.

Walking back out of the porth, a smaller version of Solva, I began to think about the old breakwater, and how it might have been built in the first place. The mystery was that the walls are built as masonry walls all the way down, and not walls built on heavy rubble, which is often the case. We soon came to our lunch stop, which was at Porth Llysgi Bay. It showed no sign of having been a harbour in the past; in fact, it can truthfully be called an idyllic place. Its small bay is divided into two beaches, with no road to either, and hence it is the very peaceful and unspoilt place we found. We made friends with a metallic green beetle, but I'm not sure whether he appreciated our company as much as we did his. Looking back towards Solva, we talked of the fine views that we'd seen through the morning, and the old postcards I'd seen, which depicted the old breakwater as it had been before it was repaired.

The gorse had not been quite as bad as it sometimes is, especially to people like ourselves, who insist on wearing shorts. It had caused discomfort of a different kind from usual, on this trip, because Joanna had insisted that the pain of being pricked by its thorns was more than she could bear, and she had to be carried through the worst parts.

As we rounded St David's Head, the view was quite dramatic; the wind had risen and the strong current flung waves and spume against the offshore rocks. We had the sudden view of Ramsey Sound and the island itself. Our main concern of the moment, however, was Joanna's blister, onto which I put a plaster dressing, which brought her much relief. There are some who say that blisters are better just left alone to heal naturally, and so encouraging a hardening of the flesh, whereas a plaster softens the skin. I've tried both but, in the short term, the plaster and its instant relief is much to be preferred, especially by our Joanna. It's worth taking note of the fact that a plaster strip should follow the line of abrasion; for example, on the back of the heel, it should be applied just vertically; that way, it's more likely to stay in place. While I was attending to my daughter, a man passed us, going in the opposite direction. He picked some blackberries, and told us that he'd just seen a seal in the cove nearby. With this news and the plaster in place, the blister was soon forgotten, and we rushed to catch our first good view of a seal.

The girls were enthralled and curious, which meant that they were very reluctant to leave. We were also longing to spend a little while at St Justinian's. I don't know why, but it just seemed to have that lingering atmosphere of childhood stories about it, and it only needed a couple of retired fishermen in Guernsey pullovers, sitting on upturned boats, to complete the Rupert Bear image. However, we had to set up our little home, in haste, at a nearby farm. The reason for the rush was simple: we couldn't wait to taste the blackberries that we'd picked on the way. Our mouths watered in anticipation of feasting on them, cooked and nestled in custard. They were delicious. Our main course consisted of curry and rice, and tea with fresh milk.

It was also good, in the especially warm evening air, to be washing and watching a classic sunset over the sea. Later in the evening, we walked down to the lifeboat station, which the girls thought looked rather eerie in the evening light. However, it had a peaceful air, and we sat on the steps, listening to the waves and watching, in the fast fading light, the powerful-looking fishing boats as they rode on their anchorage. Once again, it was hard to imagine the treachery of these waters, which make landings on Ramsey possible only at certain times of the year. At the time we were there, the island was for sale. We had been given the figure of two hundred and fifty thousand pounds, which seemed too cheap, even then, for two farms and your own little kingdom. We finally watched with interest the flashes of a lighthouse on the other side of Ramsey, and observed the mysterious sounds and movements of a tractor on the island. It occurred to us that night, that the weather had been too good to be true. In fact, we hadn't had a wet day since our first day's back-packing in North Wales. However, we weren't complaining as we got into bed at twenty to ten; we were feeling very pleased with our choice of walk.

It was a demonstration of super efficiency the next morning, when we were on parade for half past eight and away by quarter past ten, and that was after there had been a heavy dew in the night, which usually necessitates a slight pause in our preparations, as we choose a drier, lighter tent. We had to make our way down to the lifeboat station in order to pick up the path again. There was a lot of boat activity down there, and it made a colourful picture in the morning sunshine. The path was a lot better here and obviously well used by holidaymakers; as if we were any different. The views of Porth Mawr, with its backdrop of deceptively high hills and low vales, and Garn Llidi, make an excellent subject for a photograph, for even the most amateur of cameramen. We had an early lunch here, at midday, followed by ice creams, and we spent a while watching the surfers, but the place seemed crowded by Pembrokeshire standards. Therefore, it wasn't with complete regret that we turned inland, to walk the road to St David's.

The road walk wasn't too bad at all. Ironically though, when we arrived in town, with its modern conveniences, we had to wait nearly two hours for the bus. However, once again it seemed pleasantly strange to be carried along, as we excitedly picked out farms where we'd stayed, or sections of the path where we had done this or that. The greatest luxury was yet to come, and that was to sit in a comfortable seat in our own car, and that is all we did for a while, because the engine failed to start. Then, I remembered that I'd removed the rotor arm, to immobilize it, before we set out.

We drove to Nolton Haven, from where we intended to make day trips along the path to Broad Haven, and back to Newgale, thus completing the St Brides Bay walk. This presented us with an enormous slice of coast to challenge our humble efforts. We were able to have some bakestones with our tea that day, because we'd thought to leave some behind in the car. For those readers who are unfamiliar with these, they are a type of flat scone, baked on a griddle or bakestone. A Welsh shepherd, whom I know fairly well, insists that they should be called backstones, although they are more commonly named welsh-cakes. They're the perfect way to carry cake in your rucksack, for a number of reasons; first, because there's no cutting required, and you have no crumbs, and so more cake and less mess. They can also double up as a pudding, when served with instant custard. They're usually eaten with butter, but we often greedily resort to jam or marmalade, as well. It's also worth knowing that you can make your own instant custard by mixing proportionate amounts of milk powder, caster sugar and custard powder, but it is recommended that one tries it at home first, to get the proportions right. That night was one when we enjoyed good washes and home comforts in our large tent, and also the smug feeling that comes with a good job well done.

The next day we were woken by the scream of a jet fighter overhead, and I wondered if that meant we were in for yet another fine day? Well, apparently it did, because we walked that day, in warm sunshine, to Broad Haven via Druidstone Haven. Along this stretch of the coast the erosion is evident in a large way. Whole sections of the cliff's edge, sometimes the size of a football pitch, have dropped a few feet. Nonetheless, with the application of some commonsense and observance of the warnings, it's quite safe, and, with the plant life being so rich on this stretch, it's a far cry from mining area subsidence. We noticed that the ship was still anchored in the bay, assuming it to be the same one as we had seen before. Whilst in Broad Haven, we all had a look at it through one of those telescopes of the sort that you put the money in, only to have it run out just when you've got used to it, and want to focus on something interesting. After a bucket-and-spade type of afternoon, we walked back, picking blackberries for tea along the way. We saw a back-packer whom we had seen previously at Porth Llysgu Bay, on Tuesday. We tried to work out his progress since then, and experienced that silent affiliation with a stranger, due to a shared interest. This is something that I suspect is rarely considered by those who are contemplating marriage, but it is so important in the long term.

The next morning, I found a fairly large sea bird huddled in the corner of the toilets. In my ignorance, I thought it was injured in some way, because it appeared so awkward and low on the ground. After coaxing him or her into a box, we took the poor creature to a cottage near Whitesands Bay, where people were asked to take birds that had been affected by oil. It was hard to imagine that it was the problem here, because, at that time, I'd never seen any sign of oil, but with all the oil refineries at Milford Haven, it was inevitable that something would happen sometime. The young girl at the house took the bird and patiently explained that it was a Manx shearwater, and we were assured that it was fine. They live on Skomer, along with puffins, and, like the puffins, they live in the ground, presumably to get away from the black-backed gull, a very large bird that kills and eats them. We were also informed that the shearwater flies at night and our friend had probably seen some light and lost his sense of direction, thus ending up, confused, where I had found him. Finally, my young instructor announced,

"I'll let him go tonight and he'll be alright."

This was my reassurance as I walked back to the car to console my family, who had become quite worried about our little invalid. This was in spite of his very raucous and unappreciative comments, in the car, on the way over, which caused us all to jump violently when it happened.

The rest of the day was split between walking the Nolton to

Newgale stretch of path, and a car trip to Fishguard. During our walking, we nearly acquired another pet, in the form of a strange and overly friendly dog. I had to take him back twice before he would give up trying to accompany us. This reminded me of Billy, a dog in Blackwell, Derbyshire, that would make friends with anyone. His problem is that, because he lives in an area popular with walkers, he ends up going in all directions and miles from home, and has to be found and fetched back. His owners have had to resort to notices explaining their plight, and they leave a length of binder twine near the notice, with which his finders can tie him up. In Fishguard, we saw a Continental-looking couple, loaded up and obviously backpacking; and this made us half wish we were still walking. Also that day, a few miles inland from Strumble Head, we saw an elderly couple with large rucksacks, looking very tanned and healthy, which assured us that we had a long way to go to reach their level of experience. After an Ice Cream day on the morrow, we'd go home to look at our slides and make plans for the next walking tour, because there was definitely going to be a next time. Now, we could hardly imagine doing anything else. We have always loved God's good earth, and the only way to see it properly is to walk, and this makes us love it all the more, and so the circle of appreciation continues.

Chapter 5

Throughout the dark, sunless, urban winter, we pondered where we might go next. Having now walked a large slice of the Pembrokeshire Coast Path, it soon occurred to us, as I'm sure it would to most people, that by taking it in sections like this, we could walk the entire coast path. It also occurred to us that, with the advantage of backpacking, the whole of the path can be walked, and not just those parts that are convenient to car access. There are the sections where it's so quiet and the silence is so overpowering, it's as if nature is really putting you in your place. It was thoughts like this that made me look at the long, lonely walk from Poppit Sands to Fishguard, but having spent the day at Tenby and seen its delights, Ruth and Joanna wanted to go on more of what they called a proper holiday, and when they found out that Tenby and Saundersfoot were on the coast path, they would settle for nothing else.

Therefore, with the starting point at Amroth and by working our way along the coast, I thought we would probably make it to St Govan's Head. The plan was to leave the car at a campsite in Amroth, and catch a bus that would bring us as near as possible to St Govan's Head. Then, the plan was to walk back to the car. We found a campsite at the top end of Amroth, and went to check on the bus times, which was quite an operation. When we did finally get the much sought after information, it appeared that the bus made a day tour of the coast, calling at all the inland villages between Amroth and Angle. In addition, there would be a few extra miles to walk, not to mention the inevitable changes of route.

Having disposed of that idea, we made our way toward St Govan's Head, in order to check on the campsite at Bosherston. There was a site for caravans marked on the map, but we could see no sign of it at all, and presumed that it must be a caravan club weekend site. Things weren't going too well, and so we just went to the site at Freshwater East, while we put up the tent and thought about it all. The farmer's wife was extremely helpful, suggesting the best buses and even offering to give us a lift down to the main road, in the morning. It had been a very full day, part of which had been spent travelling from home. With the day off tomorrow, it being Sunday and having even fewer buses, we decided it would do best to make a fresh start on Monday. In the early evening, we walked down to the beach, amid a chorus of grasshoppers, and tasted again the real reason for our being here, the sheer magic of that boundary between land and sea.

It was probably the events of that evening, and our seeing the lighthouses, along with the rekindled memories, that prompted our quick decision in the morning to pack up and just be off to Amroth, and to forget all about buses and overlapping timetables. After taking down the big tent and sorting out our gear, it was twelve forty-five before we finally got away. Our indecision lasted while we waited in the toilets for a rainstorm to pass over. We were also delayed by having to go down to the beach shop, which was amusingly called the Lake-side Stores, where Joanna had spotted a deluxe pair of flip-flops. I couldn't complain too loudly about that, though, because I also caused a delay, when I had to go back to look for the salt I thought I'd lost from an open rucksack pocket, only to find it in the other pocket. It was now fifteen minutes past one, but, as it happened, the rain had stopped by the time we started, and we had a good day.

The headlands are sometimes very wild and, literally, breathtaking, due to high winds. We therefore very much welcomed a cup of tea at Manorbier beach. This brought back to mind a thesis I had read, on the development and decline of the English tea rooms, and their replacement by the coffee bar. We now had before us a hot dog van, similar to the many caravans that give similar service from lay-bys along most major motor routes. It represented perfectly the change from damask tablecloths to Formica table-tops, and from the sound of tinkling teacups to that of clunking mugs. Now, alas, it had deteriorated from Formica tops to flooded trays and from mugs to finger-burning plastic beakers. Fortunately, however, the liquid therein remained the same, an infusion that makes the heart of mortal man rejoice. The children had coke.

When she saw the castle, Joanna refused to believe that anyone could still be living there, but it is inhabited and has a homely appearance, especially the garden, compared with other castles we have seen. In some rooms, which are lit up, and can look a little eerie, it has life-size models to illustrate its unusual history. There was much information of general interest, but, on that windy day, it was hard to imagine that the valley below once supported a vineyard. In those days of hard work for some and wealth for a few, life and outlook must have been very different from what they are today, and the weather was different from now, as well.

As we walked back from the beach, our history lesson continued when we saw an ancient quoit, or mini Stonehenge, right on the edge of the path. In fact, I leant on it, to have a rest, and wondered why it had been built so near to the edge of the cliff, and, more especially, how it was still there, in view of the large fissures in the rocks nearby, which suggest that there must have been severe movement in the past. Around the point, in spite of the path being well used, it seemed remote and peaceful. A strolling couple stopped and commented on the coastal beauty, and then asked us about St David's, which made our heads swell a bit, as we were able to speak knowingly about various parts of the path and the surrounding area. Then, with a jolt, I remembered humbly how privileged I was to be there, free to choose where I walk, well almost free. I say that because we were to come up against our first incidence of access denied, at Old Castle Head. This land, adjacent to the nearby army camp, is one of the many tracts of good land used by the Military. I call it good land partly because these military sites are usually in areas of outstanding beauty, but also because they were in use pre-war, and are therefore free of insecticide and other agricultural cocktails. We camped in a farmer's field near here, because it was almost five o'clock. It was sensible to stop while we could; it was unlikely that we would find another site quickly. In the evening, the clouds were very red. A red sky at night was supposed to presage fine weather.

It rained slightly during the night, and we had groans to air in the morning, about ploughs that caught headlands and harrows that missed them. So much for soothsaying shepherds. However, I don't think it was that which caused us to be up at seven o'clock, to discover a fine day. We were away by ten to nine, after breakfasting on particularly good muesli. We have found that our own homemade muesli works out very successfully. We purchase a muesli base from a health food shop; add to that chopped nuts, even peanuts, oats, raisins, crushed bran and soft brown sugar. In addition to this, you can add crisp-bread and cracker crumbs as you go along. To this you add some milk powder and water. It's better than the good old standby porridge, because there's no dirty billycan to be scrubbed, and you can make do with a cold water wash-up, without having to wait for water to heat. As well as saving gas, a breakfast of muesli means that we all get away a bit earlier. This brings to mind the old Alpine saying, "There's no substitute for an early start." How true that is, in many aspects of life. However, although we were on the road early that morning, it was still a far cry from the three-thirty rise of a sage who lives in an alpine hut.

With the need to walk around Lydstep Point, as well as the pleasant diversion of exploring Lydstep Caverns, we seemed to be getting nowhere for a while. We were rewarded with the special joy of being on Lydstep beach in the sun at lunchtime. It was an especially cheeky joy, because Lydstep is a private beach, with no public access. However, the coast path runs straight across it, and so, once again, we mere walkers enjoyed special privileges. The views of Caldy Island are particularly good from this area, the island's beaches looking very exotic as they shone unspoilt and reflecting the hot summer sun. We also saw the boats going around Caldy, reminding us of when we ourselves had gone round it in search of seals. To get out of Lydstep beach proved to be quite a problem as we could find no definite coast path leaving the beach, and when we ended up in a maze of caravans and sandy-toed children, we began to despair. We didn't want to bring any reproach on future walkers, but it just didn't seem possible to find any logical route to the cliff tops. It was, therefore, with a great sense of relief that our rucksacks were dropped on the elusive path's verge, when we at last made it back to the cliff tops. We looked back and marvelled at how much time and effort it had taken to get from just over there to over here.

Once again, the butterflies were all around us; I recalled that my father used to call them flutterbies. There were also some large, green, furry caterpillars, and all conversation stopped as soon as one was spotted, and we'd stare at it, entranced. I presume that, in my father's terminology, he would call them patterkillers.

Now, due to the sudden change in the area's rock type, there was a great change in the scenery. From old sandstone, it changes to that prince of rocks, carboniferous limestone. The views of these rock bastions were further enhanced by the presence of seemingly wild horses, grazing the open headland pastures. Suddenly, much to the alarm of Ruth and Joanna, the peace of the afternoon was broken by the distant sound of rifle shots. It took a lot to convince Joanna that, if we followed the instructions on the notices, and walked close to the fence, we'd be perfectly safe. Through the gate she slunk, and started to stalk warily down the field. Ruth's nerves also showed signs of cracking, as both she and Joanna kept telling me that I was over the suggested limit, even though I was no more than the stipulated six feet away from the fence. Joanna looked back and noticed the sentry peep out from his box at us, which made her feel even worse and convinced her that we were all doomed. Then, we walked on to the bottom end of the field, and inland. At the bottom was another sentry box but with no peeping soldier. As we approached it, the sentry appeared and watched us walk by and out onto the road. I wondered afterwards whether the one had informed the other of the possible invasion by our family.

The site at Penally was excellent, with all the luxuries that we'd missed the night before. It was also near to the village, and a large and beautiful beach, where we went for a walk during the evening, which turned out unusually warm and calm. Penally must be one of the few villages left in this country that has its own halt or railway station. We had to cross the line to reach the beach. On our way back from the beach, we watched the train, moving like a silver worm crawling through the night; it stopped at the little platform to the sound of steam brakes and slamming carriage doors. Accentuated by the dramatic lighting, the scene prompted a flood of memories. Vividly I recalled childhood train journeys, on our way to visit distant aunts, waiting on unlit, dark platforms, in the hush of the night, for that haven of warmth and activity to appear through the gloom.

On arrival at our destination, the train's motherly figure disappeared into the night, and the last we saw of it was its red rear lamp. We would be left in this dark, silent emptiness, and had to try to find our out of the station.

Meanwhile, back in Penally, we went back over the crossing and returned to the tent, where we sat in the tent doorway, reluctant to go to bed, saying how nice it would be to stop here for a few days and nurse Judith's weary limbs. It had been a good day, and now we wanted an extension.

The next morning, which was Tuesday, we were away by 9.40. Going over the railway crossing again, we found a third sentry on duty and asked about whether we would be safe if we used the path, which passes across the firing range. The range was in operation by the time we arrived, without being wounded, on the beach. This is reputedly a beach where Winston Churchill spoke to the troops as they trained for D-day. We had turned and begun to walk along this beach in the direction of Tenby, when we got the thing we had feared for so long: it began to rain. We sheltered, while we got out our long unused cagoules, and folded leggings for Ruth and Joanna, who had insisted on wearing trousers. Even with the rain, we still enjoyed the walk through Tenby.

While one guarded the rucksacks, which we dumped down on the very narrow pavement, the other went into a shop, to buy fresh bread baps and iced buns. Further on, we stopped outside a fashionable, old fashioned grocery shop, to buy some pâté. Every time we stopped for shopping, we had to take our rucksacks off, and when we set off again, we had to haul them back on, always being careful not to injure any innocent passers-by.

We made our way around to the North Beach, intending to enjoy that great British summer pastime of sitting in a large seaside shelter and devouring our lunch. However, we had to wait our turn for a seat until others moved on. Then, we enjoyed our food, seated amid a crowd of pensioners, most of who seemed to be on a trip. Their conversation was animated and they didn't seem to complain or joke about the weather too much. Perhaps they just appreciated the fact they were there, instead of sat at home and staring out at the rain. Some complaining couples came and went, but our little haven of good natured people managed to stay intact. One elderly lady gave Ruth and Joanna a packet of crisps, assuring us that she didn't want them herself. Her kindness was typical of her generation; she had learned the joy that unselfish giving can bring.

Among those that dropped in out of the rain were the two backpackers that we'd seen previously; they gave a knowing nod, although we were strangers, and passed on. Their kindness was a little more subtle, but apparent nonetheless. However, there was no kindness in the rain, which came on even harder before we finally moved ourselves, and set off up the appropriately named Waterwynch Lane, which leads out of Tenby towards Saundersfoot.

In spite of the rain, we could appreciate how lush and verdant the land was on either side, and, in good weather, no doubt it would be a fine place for observing wildlife, but on a day like today, the animals had more sense than to come out of their lairs. The hedges meet at the top of the path, and this arching tunnel succeeded in giving us some shelter, but it wasn't long before we discovered that

Joanna's cagoule had passed its prime, which is generally the trouble with lightweight, water-proofed nylon. I had some dustbin liners in my rucksack, out of which we fabricated a waterproof lining for her cagoule, and devised a hood out of one corner. I cut appropriate holes for her face and arms. I also discovered that I'd left my rucksack pocket open. Fortunately, nothing was lost, or overly wet.

The only people we met on this dismal day must have been as mad as ourselves. First, we passed some girls, who looked very wet and poorly equipped. One had a tidy camera, just dangling from her rucksack, all open to the weather, which made me wince. However she didn't seem at all bothered, not even when I pointed it out. Then, the backpacking pair, who had nodded to us earlier in the shelters, overtook us. Once again, they smiled, and just briefly asked, "Couldn't you sit it out any longer?"

At this stage of the walk, the tall hedges had changed and become lush, dense and reminiscent of tropical forests. This, along with thick sea mist, very much restricted our views that day, although we did manage to see Monkstone Point and its adjacent beach, far below the cliff path, before we went back into the woods, and followed a path that led up to Saundersfoot.

We discovered an old mineshaft in these woods, an adit that ran down, at a 45 degree angle, into the solid rock. This was a grim reminder of Saundersfoot's mining history. We also discovered another equipment casualty. Ruth's waterproof had ripped under the arm, and we were thankful to have with us some repair tape, which we used to prevent the seam ripping further. As I repaired it, I realised that the rain had stopped, which was just as well, because we still had a fair way to go.

It was while we were in the woods, that we heard the wind blow through the tops of the trees. It sounded just like a plane going swiftly overhead. Alas, this was not our speed of travel, and we had an awkward decision to make: whether to walk on to Amroth, or walk inland and find a suitable campsite. We chose the latter, but didn't bargain for the uphill drag, every step of which we begrudgingly trudged. We knew that we would have to retrace our steps on the following morning. But, with the tent up, and every wet thing hanging out to dry in the late afternoon sunshine, it seemed to have been worth it. The campsite proved to be the usual source of fresh food and cheap toys. However, before the shop opened, we had our tea, a strange mixture of macaroni, shrimps and rice, followed by bakestones and custard. To find ourselves sitting down to a meal at 5.30 meant we were becoming quite civilised, and it was a real luxury to be without the rain.

I woke very early the next morning, to the sound of someone whispering in my ear.

"Terry! There's water dripping on my face."

I shot upright and grabbed hold of the torch, which I shone around the tent. The whole of the interior was covered with droplets of water. Still half asleep, I looked outside, and saw a cloudless, starry sky overhead. I was completely baffled. In my stupor, I decided that the droplets must be the result of heavy dew, and the tent cloth, having been dry for so long, hadn't yet swollen enough to waterproof itself.

Then, for some reason that I was unable to fathom, the water started dripping everywhere, and so I hurriedly put the girls' sleeping bags inside dustbin liners, moved things away from the walls, into bags and off the floor. Afterwards, I simply laid myself down again, and let it continue to drip.

It all seemed like a dream, when we awoke at 7.15. The sun came out and efficiently dried the tent and sundry other sodden items, and we were off back to Saundersfoot by 10.30. It was certainly a lot easier going back downhill, and we soon found ourselves browsing through the shops. On the way out of town, we found a lovely little bookshop, where I could have stopped for hours, but we went through the old railway arch, and came to a small but crowded beach. At one stage, Joanna was reluctant to go through the old, narrow, four-foot gauge tunnels, which some children would find as much fun as having a fairground on the beach. In this area, there are many ongoing improvements to cater for the holiday crowds, including the path we now walked.

Another change has been an enlargement of the pub at Wiseman's Bridge. It still stands where it has always stood, but it has been extended once, and enlarged and extended again, and the old smugglers' inn has been almost completely swallowed up.

The lane behind the pub led uphill again, and we followed it until we came out onto the path proper. We sat down on the side of the path, and spread out our gear, ready to enjoy our lunch of cobs, pâté, tomatoes, crisps and apples. Then, suddenly, it all had to be packed away again, as it started to rain. In fact, the whole procedure from now on seemed rather like the way out we had come out of Tenby, only now it was in reverse.

High-topped hedges and woodland led us very suddenly down to Amroth, and Joanna found it difficult to accept this sudden end to our expedition. To follow the Tenby pattern, we finished our lunch in a bus shelter. This time, we were sharing it with a very young family, who were feasting on chips. Suddenly, there was the bus, and we were diverted by all the hurly-burly of finding money for our fares, and getting our pile of belongings on board. We sat back and watched as the villages passed us by. It was as if we were watching our path as a video, fast action replay.

We had to change buses in Tenby, where we had rather a long wait and so we had another meal, and ate it in a shelter on the seafront. We had another bus change to make, at the army camp, and we walked the last couple of up-hill miles to the car, which we had left at the farm at Freshwater East. After thanking the more than helpful farmer's wife, we made our way back to Penally, to enjoy hot showers, soft beds and a real potato stew.

Over the next few days, we finished off the little bits of the walk that we'd previously missed out, such as the last half-mile at Amroth, and we enjoyed the intoxicating evening air at Giltar Point. At first, it seemed a little absurd to go there at that time of day, but when we saw Caldy and St Margaret's Isle in the moonlight, we considered ourselves very fortunate to have been there on that occasion. The last half-mile at Amroth was different and very perfunctory. We were a little disappointed that no definite sign marked the end to the coast path. In fact, we walked on up the lane, past the fictitious boundary. While we expected no brass band, a formal type photo at the official end would have been nice.

Chapter 6

To date, we had walked 75 miles of the 168 miles of peaceful coastal beauty, and could now see that the opportunity to explore its whole length was within our grasp, just by taking little bites at it during future holidays, taking care not to miss any little bits. Many who walk sections, but who start from where they have parked their car, will more than likely omit the same little bits, which, accordingly, become the least walked and, hence, the best.

Our choice was now becoming greatly reduced. We only had three stretches left to suit our holiday walking pattern of one week with a few days off. These sections were St Dogmaels to Fishguard, Fishguard to Whitesands Bay, and the walk round Milford Haven, from Dale to Freshwater East.

On cold winter nights, when we sat around the fire, or during one-day and weekend walks in Derbyshire, we discussed our strategy for the coming year. The Derbyshire landscape certainly sparked our enthusiasm, and we found ourselves even talking seriously of walking the Pennine Way, using our new found key to long distance walking. Joanna was amazed to think you could walk to Scotland from where we stood, in Edale. It was interesting how everyone had earlier been keen to be in the holiday area of Tenby, and yet now we craved the windswept and deserted headlands, and the northern reach of the Pembrokeshire walk began to beckon.

Whilst I didn't really want to leave the Milford stretch till last, we couldn't resist the Fishguard area, and it was decided that we would walk the two parts, either side of Fishguard, in a fortnight holiday. This was quite a brave undertaking for us, because there were many little problems, due to the short daily mileage we could manage with the girls. There were too few campsites, and we would have to resort to using the youth hostels, which served this part of the coast quite well, especially the leg from Fishguard to St David's. However, even then, there were still places where we just hoped to be able to camp somewhere.

As part of the preparation, and as a result of last year's wet chapter, we also bought another tent. This now gave us two small tents, and we bought a proper rucksack for Ruth. We needed to get hold of another map, as the northern stretch of our walks would be on the Cardiganshire map. We started stocking up with dehydrated foods and collecting suitable polythene bags. We decided to buy new cagoules for us all, which was quite an expense, as some of them were made of Gore-Tex, a wonderful material, with no sign of condensation, even when the wearer is in low gear and carrying a full load uphill. It's laughable, when I think about how we prepare for yesterday, and bar the stable door after the horse has bolted. In any event, we were better equipped for this year than we had been for last year.

When I looked at Ruth's bigger rucksack, it gave me reason to reflect on how different things used to be, when the girls were smaller and came on their first walks with us. It was a pleasant, natural progression, that as our gear grew in weight so did our carrying capacity. The burden of yesteryear, if they'll forgive me for my calling them that, had become a burden-bearer.

I'm not sure whether it was due to our enthusiasm to get started, but at 8 o'clock on the Saturday morning, we were at Devils Bridge, looking for a toilet. Then, by 11 o'clock, we were at Poppitt Sands Youth Hostel, and that was in spite of taking time out to do some shopping. To celebrate our arrival, we spent the afternoon on the beach. The tents were pitched in amongst the bracken, in front of the Hostel, on a piece of land that was normally kept clear by a grazing goat. We waited apprehensively for our first Hostel to open, which should have been at five o'clock. I had spoken to the warden earlier about pitching the tent and booking in. Then, just before five, the girls and I collected together our food, pans and cups etc, along with our stove, and marched up to the hostel kitchen. We were completely green as far as hostels are concerned, and didn't realize that so much was laid on for visitors, even for us, mere tramping campers, who only have to pay half the adult hostel fee.

The children went running back to the tents, whooping for joy, to tell mum that there were cookers, teapots, plates and cutlery, even an electric kettle. A demonstration of the good nature of the warden was found in the provision of a tray, complete with electric kettle, milk, sugar, tea bags and cups, along with a notice saying, "Hope you had a nice day. Have a cup on me."

It certainly seemed odd to stand at a cooker and sit down at a table, while back-packing, and, afterwards, to wash up at a sink with running hot water. We all solemnly declared hostelling to be, as Paddington Bear might say, "Very good value for money". It was also very refreshing, after a long, hard day spent on our feet.

We sat in comfortable chairs in the evening, which is always a luxury that we do without when micro-camping. We read, played chess, dominoes and even did a bit to a jigsaw. Despite the fact that the afternoon had turned misty, the evening was clear and full of beauty. There were porpoises swimming in the bay, and the warden told us that they would normally put on a better display. Things seemed to be going right, even to the point of there being no midges, in spite of the thick bracken. But the map on the wall reminded me of the serious walk in front of us, and I still hadn't seen a map of the stretch of path that ran from here to Newport and Parrog, which was approximately fourteen miles away and would take us over fairly rough ground. I studied the map and tried to glean all the information I could, and then implant it within my reluctant mind. I was desperately hoping to find somewhere to camp near Ceibwr, or Pwll-y-wrach, which was only just over six miles away.

That night, the warden introduced me to a farmer, with whom I made some prior arrangements for parking the car. Then we spent a funny half hour, trying to find the washroom for Judith and the girls; all of us were afraid to go in anywhere, in case it proved to be the wrong room. Going back to the tent, Joanna informed us that she very much wanted to sleep in one of those lovely little beds, referring to the beds she had seen in the hostel. She thought it would be very much worth the extra money, and she implored me to agree to this, at the next hostel we visited. While I didn't actually agree, she took my grunted answer for agreement, and contentedly snuggled down as deep as she could into her thin Karrimat.

The dawn was an exciting one, with mist drifting down the estuary below us, and then on out to sea. We could vaguely see the line of Poppit Sands, but above the mist on the other side, the fields could be clearly seen in the crisp morning light. This hostel provided us with the luxury of toast and jam, as seconds for breakfast. This was quite something, as toast had been one thing that I'd always craved while camping. After revelling in these little treats, the warden gave us the task of raking off the trimmings of a previous day's mowing, on the very steep ground to the side of the hostel, which must, I suppose, rank as the front lawn. These grass cuttings would be used eventually to feed or bed the resident goat. Our full task also involved the application of shears to an overgrown bush. I sometimes wonder whether it recovered afterwards. We did get going eventually, by half past eleven, and parked the car where we had arranged to leave it, at the farm, where we briefly spoke to an elderly lady, who was Welsh-speaking. This, I suspect, was something unusual in this Little England beyond Wales, where even the Welsh accent is now uncommon.

Just past the farmhouse, we crossed our first stile. It was clearly marked with the number four hundred and seventy-eight, which we

We'd soon knocked off ten stiles

assumed indicated the number of stiles between here and Amroth, this being the last of them all. The direction in which we intended to travel was the wrong one, in the magical world of officialdom. The scenery around the hostel had reminded us of the coast near Howelston, but once we were past Cemaes Head, the change was very pronounced. Here its famous rock strata became evident, looking very much like the cross-section of a petrified wave.

I smiled to myself, when I spotted the coastguard's lookout here. It was full of hay, evidence of the local farmer's resourcefulness. It also caused me to think of the path itself, wearily and faithfully trodden by coastguards in the past, long before the right of way movements of the Second World War No doubt, they spent many a lonely and dangerous night, walking the ways we now walk for pleasure. This is true, I'm sure, of the drove roads and what are now termed green lanes, though, with the current interest in off-road-driving, they're fast becoming brown lanes again.

At Ceibwr Bay we saw a family who'd been camped next to us at the hostel, and had been given the job of leading the goat to pastures anew. We also saw a lot of other people, which came as a bit of a shock after the solitude on the path. However, we could see no sign of any possible campsite or likely farm; in fact, we couldn't even envisage camping wild. This is where I probably began to make some wrong decisions. There was water here, but no likely campsite, and so we were to walk on and look for a suitable unofficial site. Unlike camping in the mountains, if you find a site in the sort of place we now found ourselves, there's probably going to be no water. Also, with not having a map for this first section I didn't fully appreciate how much farther it was to Newport. I had been thinking that Ceibwr Bay was halfway, when it wasn't at all.

We went trudging on, in the vain hope of finding what we

needed. Along this stretch there are lots of knobbly bits of rock; arches and caves, but first prize goes to Pwll-y-Wrach, or the Witch's Cauldron. It was a maze of arches and caves, and huge. We would loved to have seen the place at high tide, or, better still, with a spring tide, however, crossing one particular arch was fearsome enough as it was. The sea must surely seem to boil at times like that, and hence the name, which we thought was so appropriate to this dark and sinister area.

Later, as we were pushing and struggling along through thick, tall ferns, it all seemed, in our tired state, like a dream. A green dream, I called it, but Ruth said it was more like a nightmare. The path seemed to go on and on, at this stage, with no sign of turn in towards the peninsula. We also dreaded encountering any drop in height, because it would mean a painful and slow climb up the other side.

When it seemed as if the path went on for ever, without an end, we stopped in the open, in spite of a breeze, on a low, sloping headland, to have a late tea. The time was 7 o'clock. Looking back on that day, I'm amazed and grateful, to remember how Ruth and Joanna kept going, especially Ruth, who was now carrying quite a substantial load. The meagre menu consisted of corned beef, which Joanna doesn't like at the best of times, two tomatoes between the four of us, cream crackers and cake; the tomatoes were our only source of liquid, our flasks being long since emptied. I thought of the warden's words.

"Oh, you should make it alright to Newport."

I wished I'd thought a bit more about them before setting off. I wished, too, that I'd bought a map. I wished we'd stopped at Ceibwr. I wished we'd started earlier. There was, however, no genie available to grant our wishes, and so we were still here, had to be there, and there was only one way to get to there.

It was nine o'clock before we saw Newport, so it did exist, after all. It was sad that, due to our current situation, we weren't fully appreciative of the many birds and fine scenery we'd seen along the way. Gulls galore had wheeled above us, some with black topped wings, one that I thought might have been a Manx shearwater, and a black and white bird with a call like a blackbird's alarm call. I also saw grey/black birds skimming over the surface of the water, so obviously these were shags or cormorants.

We came down onto the beach at Newport, where the toilets were still open, and we thirstily drank water in the fast fading light. There were some people camping near the beach; one individual was most concerned about the condition of the path, and kept asking questions. He was, astonishingly, tackling it on a bicycle. I really couldn't see the sense of dragging a useless machine along the path, and couldn't imagine him cycling along some of the steeper or more awkward stretches.

We resisted the temptation to camp there ourselves, and decided to move on along the path, which takes a long and tortuous detour inland at this point, to get to the bridge over the estuary. Walking along, with even the half-light fast disappearing, I noticed that the mud flats were covered with hundreds of birds. Were they lapwings, I asked myself. It was difficult to be sure, what with the encroaching darkness and my extreme tiredness.

When, finally, the bridge was reached, the girls sat down in total despair. They realised that we would now have to walk the same distance down the other side of the estuary, and still have to find a campsite, in addition to all that, it was already ten o'clock at night. We walked down a lane with high hedges either side, which made it almost too dark to see at all. We came out onto the road, where I asked the first man I saw, in case there wasn't another one about so late at night, if he knew of a campsite that we could get to before everyone would be gone to bed. He pointed to a woman walking on the other side of the street, and said that we should ask her. However, as I thanked him and raced after her, she vanished down an alleyway. With yours truly in as hot a pursuit as I could muster, I became afraid that she was going to think the worst. I had mad visions of her running off, screaming, but, contrary to that, she asked us to come in to her house. I asked her about the chances of us finding a campsite. She brushed my concern aside, said that there was a site nearby, and insisted that we would be alright. Would this weird day never end?

She then gave us cups of tea, while we sat in her kitchen, hearing stories of the family's barbecue that night, and a beautiful pet donkey they used to have. Photographs of him and their extended family were affectionately passed around, as if we were some visiting relatives. It was then that I saw, in the brightness of the electric light, how tired Judith and the girls really were, and I was, therefore, pleased when the woman's husband led us through their beautiful garden, beyond which lay a real campsite, complete with a brand new, stylish toilet block. It was almost incredible to believe our good fortune, as we passed through into the darkness of this other world. I felt a little embarrassed by his kindness, as he held the torch for us while we put up the tents. He regaled us with stories from the area's long history of smuggling. Even recently, fibreglass bunkers and marine engines had, apparently, been found in many of the caves of the area. He also spoke of twenty-foot-high waves in the winter, which one would expect to wash the whole village away. Nevertheless, the thought of all that water didn't stop me drinking a lot more water, before we finally collapsed into blissful bed, at gone midnight.

The next day was Monday, August the first, and a holiday for us. I'd faithfully promised the girls that there would be no walking that day because we had, in effect, done two day's walking yesterday, according to our low mileage schedules. In fact, I tried to make it even more of a holiday for all by serving cups of tea in bed. They had breakfast in the same location, and soon began to revel in the joy of there being no walking that day. I also felt an enormous sense of relief, knowing that the most awkward stretch was over. Even so, it was sad that we hadn't had more time to enjoy this more majestic part of the kingdom. It seemed so wild, without being a wilderness. One guidebook describes the stretch from Pwll-y-Wrach to Newport as one of the best solitary walks in the country. We thought that was very much the best understatement in the book.

In the morning, we bought some salad for lunch, as well as some postcards and chocolate from a beach café. After lunch, which was an opportunity to indulge in plenty of tea, the bright lights of Newport beckoned. We bought yet more food, as well as another film for our camera. The children were given an inflatable beach ball, which can be let down so as to fit into their rucksack. On the way up to the shops, a woman on the opposite side of the road tripped and fell over. We wanted to go over and see if she was all right and yet, we held back for fear of causing her any embarrassment. In the end, I just called across, asking if she were all right. She very candidly said that it was her own fault for being so nosey. She went on to explain how she'd thought we looked such a nice family group, and being thus engrossed with us, she missed her step, or, should I say, she caught a step in the path. This was another of those incidents that happened to us along the way that caused us to reflect again about our choice of walking path through life, with our progeny in tow. That woman had caught us ambling up the street, with a child apiece, arm in arm. We hoped we would continue to be blessed with the ability to keep the parent-child communication gap at bay as the dreaded teenage years approached.

Back at Parrog, we sat in a shelter, drinking cans of cola, orange and shandy. Obviously we were making up for lost time after yesterday, and we most certainly enjoyed our quick macaroni and Chicken Supreme for tea. After the leisurely day, I had a relaxed chat with our next-door neighbour, if we can use that expression about someone lodging in the tent next to ours. The whole place did seem to have a suburban air. The man spoke of the glories of Strumble Head, where we had yet to go, while I answered his questions about the Marloes-Dale peninsula, where he and his wife hoped to go tomorrow.

It had been a beautifully pleasant day, and we all vividly remember looking at a huge, dense, white cloud, shaped like a chef's hat, it seemed so dense, and yet, in its purity of whiteness, it formed a real dream topping of a cloud. It also seemed hard to really comprehend the thousands of tons of water it so silently and effortlessly carried. The evening was spent with games of cards, and plasters were placed on blisters, in preparation for tomorrow. I also had to reassure Joanna, who was worried that it might turn out to be another exhausting day, like Sunday. As if that were possible!

Chapter 7

We rose at about a quarter to eight. While rolling up our beds before breakfast, I noticed that our neighbours were also making preparations to depart. They had far more to sort out by way of worldly goods than we mere vagabonds, or, as one man that I worked with said;

"The more you have, the more you have to worry about."

Before we set out, at eleven o'clock, I had to put a plaster on Joanna's blister. Blisters are not normally a problem, except when boots are new. Nonetheless, I still had to pad her boot with some card later, so as to stop the chafing of her boot seam.

As we were walking through the outlying houses of Parrog, we could well imagine its smuggling past, in this very quiet part of the country, and also imagine the twenty-foot seas running up this side of the bay. After we had crossed our first stile, we felt as if we'd really started on the next leg of our journey. This stile bore the number four hundred and thirty-three, which, according to my arithmetic, meant that we had, amazingly, clambered over forty-five stiles on Sunday. Certainly, that emphasized the distance we had covered, more than the actual length of the walk as indicated by the map, and on the traditional day of rest, at that.

Now, we began to feel the benefit of our rest. In fact, we all felt quite recovered, and very much in the right mood to enjoy a quiet lunch at Aberhigian, among some upturned boats. Here was another quiet little beach, which, until the advent of the motor car, must have indeed been remote and known to only a few, because, even today, at the peak of the holiday season, we had it to ourselves. We climbed back up onto the headlands again, to look down on the rocks below. We saw something there that compelled us to take a second, longer look. Below us, jammed on the rocks, was an empty motor launch. Our immediate reaction was to wonder what it was doing there, and where were its occupants. It just sat there, occasionally bumping about in the surf, as if trying to free itself from a situation that has been the death of many a fine vessel. I shuddered to think what the continual bumping was doing to its fibreglass hull. Whilst time and tide wait for no man, it also has no respect for the current price of boats, or the value of its contents. There was nothing we could do from this spot on the top of a sheer cliff, and the only thing we thought it reasonable to do was to look out for some boat-type people, and speak to them about our find, at the next opportunity.

I have subsequently wondered what the legal situation would have been, had we been able to reach the launch and board it. It's certainly true that bad news travels fast, because, as we were coming down into Aber-Fforest, we saw some boats in the water, and thought that we should report our find to someone there, but just then, a lad came into view, walking quickly across the beach, and onto the path towards us. As I asked him if he knew anyone who'd lost a boat, a look of relief came over his face, as he breathlessly described the same craft that we had spotted. Tired though he must have been, he shot off up the path. He ran on, continuing to express gratitude to us and his maker. I did wonder what good he could do from up there, but by the time we had got down onto the beach, the boy's father was bringing the boat in, towed by another. Watching them bring it in toward the beach, we could see the lad we'd been speaking to up on the cliff-top. He was on the boat. How he'd got down so quickly, I have no idea, although he looked wet enough to have dived in. It looked a comparatively easy job to bring the launch in over the swell, but it would have been a much different proposition had the hull been punctured. We could well imagine their relief, as we left them to sort out the details of what had happened.

As we came out onto the lane that leads appealingly down into Cwm-Yr-Eglwys, our concern was the time of day and where we might find our next campsite. We debated whether to walk through Cwm Dewi, or go around Dinas Head. I asked some young people who were passing by, if they could tell me about any campsites in the area. They told us that there was one at Dinas, which was a little way inland, but they didn't know about Pwll Gwaelod, on the other side of Cwm Dewi. Apparently, this valley, many years ago, was a sea strait, and Dinas was an island. We were surprised at the crowd of people we encountered in Cwm-Yr-Eglwys, but this was due to there being a local water-sports-day, presumably a school event. We eagerly took advantage of the ice cream van. We also marvelled at the dramatic contrast between the laughter of children, the warm sunshine and the calm waters, set against the grim remains of the ruined church. This ruin is a stark reminder of the storm of 1859, which is reported to have dragged all but one wall into the very same water that lapped so peacefully, that day, on the man-made rock pool. The pool was complete with swimming lanes and diving boards. I've since been told that a second storm came and washed away the graveyard, complete with its occupants.

Returning to our more mundane problems, I asked a second group of young lads, who looked as though they could be local, whether there was a campsite at Bryn Henllan. Their answers mystified us considerably. One said that there was no site, then they had a discussion, and another said,

"You'll see the tents when you get to Pwll Gwaelod."

On that note, we went off to enjoy the views from Dinas Head. This spot is a good bit higher than the rest of the cliff path, and it juts well out into the sea. These features make it an ideal viewing point from which to scan the water to Newport and beyond, and we began to pick out various lunch spots, and other highlights, that we had experienced along our way, in the course of past excursions. To look the opposite way was to look into the future, a little vague at present, with unfulfilled promises and nagging apprehension. We could see Fishguard in the distance, and a cliff top caravan site, a good few miles farther on, but as yet, we could see no tents close by. After losing height rapidly, we came down to the Sailor's Safety Inn and asked a man, who was leaning on a gate, whether there was any camp site handy.

"Just walk up the valley and pick a spot," he said. "Everyone else does."

We did just that. But what a place it was! There were tents there that looked as if they had been there all summer, with garden walls, paths, dogs and Siamese cats, all giving a sense of homely permanence. The public toilets also proved to be the site facilities, and the pub and restaurant completed a recreational retreat, catering for a very unusual clientele. We sat outside and marvelled at this weird wonderland, in which we found ourselves drinking shandy and eating crisps. We now understood exactly what those boys had meant, when they said there was no campsite but we'd find the place by the tents that were there. We also understood the wry smile of the man on the gate as we walked back down, who reappeared later, and asked us if we had found a suitable place.

"Quite a place, isn't it?" he said, smiling. "They all keep coming back; some have been coming here for twenty years."

We could well believe it. This narrow strip of land, which had once belonged to the sea, had become a paradise to those who had discovered it. It certainly appeared to be a very welcome haven, far from normal, everyday, mundane life, with the Sailor's Safety Inn acting as the hostel from Wonderland.

The leisurely air must have affected us, because we weren't up until a quarter past eight the following morning, but we still got away for a quarter past eleven, on yet another fine day. Our smiling friend was there again, near the pub, as if he was waiting to escort us out of this magic-spot, which would vanish as soon as we were gone. After a polite morning nod, we soon found ourselves on the coast path again, which proved to be much quieter than Dinas Head.

Lunch that day was consumed at Hescwm, where the path takes a very short detour inland and we had to make our way up a lane, to gain the necessary height, before coming onto the cliff top again. It was here that we passed a pig farm, with its fields denuded of grass, while, on the path, the luxuriance of vegetation was literally overwhelming. To what extent the pigs were responsible we could but tentatively surmise.

Stepping out onto the top was like stepping out onto a stage, while the drama was all around us, with clear water and sharp cliff views, seen through crisp clear air. Our backdrop of lush, warm, Pembrokeshire countryside went unnoticed, as the orchestra played on the rocks below. At this point, we marvelled at how the bays succeeded one another, as if they were being made on some creative production line. Each one was different from the rest, a one off. However, these are not just views or vistas, in the way that the Victorian gentry saw them, because, as you walk round and through this three-dimensional world, the other senses make it live. A small bay is truly beautiful, but when a gull sails into it, its moaning cry echoing off the cliffs below, you really become aware of this as a living landscape. It was here also that yet another couple asked us how far we had walked, and with miles in a day now occasionally reaching double figures, our modest reply was beginning to sound quite impressive, while, in reality, it was relatively modest.

With leopard-coloured butterflies moving along in front of us, we soon arrived at the cliff top caravan site, which would be our night's stop, after a short-walk day. Everything about our stop here seemed so refreshing. Firstly, we had the extra time to enjoy the afternoon, which was still sunny and warm. Secondly, a shower, which is always refreshing, appeared to be sheer bliss, that day. Then, with the comfortable feel of clean clothes on our backs, we went to the site shop, where, apart from the usual sustenance, Ruth and Joanna bought a torch.

Back at our temporary home, at the tent, we found that the people in the next tent were packing up and making ready to go home for real, which seemed a little odd, so late in the day. Whilst the mother very kindly gave us some milk they had left over, the grown daughter continued to sunbathe outside, seemingly determined to take home the last drop of sun. After enjoying our chicken roll salad, we went up to enjoy what must be the ultimate luxury in backpacking. We sat in large armchairs, a luxury in itself, watching some action adventure in the television lounge, which, incidentally, is next door to an excellent launderette. With a sunset view through the window, we wished all Wednesdays could be like this one, leisurely and full.

The next day saw us packed and away for half past ten, headed towards Fishguard, passing on the way a rock, which was shaped exactly like the eye of a needle. This, we found out later, was called

Needle Rock. We also noticed the Irish ferry coming in during the course of the morning, as it did on a regular basis. It started to rain while we were here but eased off by the time we had arrived at Fishguard's old fort, where we spoke to a couple that we'd met briefly a couple of days earlier. I couldn't be sure, but it was either at Aber-Fforest or Pont-y-Meddig. It's a bit difficult to remember sometimes, as the many beaches and bays tend to run one into the other, or end up in the wrong order, in my memory. Despite the loss of this detail, I can still vividly remember the man, sitting director-style in a chair of a similar quality, on the grass bank that tops the beach. He had told us that he was a schoolteacher, and we envied the extra walking time that he and his wife would have available to them through their long holiday. Such long holiday breaks make single-trip, long-distance paths a comfortable possibility. They told us about the cottage where they were staying, and how their young landlady had fed them so well, with the emphasis on country fare. She was obviously one of the back to the soil, brown bread and sugar brigade. Apparently, they even used a horse and cart, instead of the usual 'twist me and go', which has changed the lives of all of us.

While we were posting our first film at the post office down at the harbour, we met the teaching couple again. After this, we walked around the harbour and up into the town itself, where we took ravenous advantage of an excellent and inexpensive café. The children and I had bacon, egg and tomatoes, while mother had TWO eggs and beans on toast. This reminded me of someone with whom I used to work. He used to describe the ideal landlady as one who greeted him in the morning with, "Good morning, Mr Waterfield, and HOW MANY eggs would you like this morning?"

Our little feast was finished off with homemade cakes and two pots of tea. The proprietor was most helpful and understanding, allowing us to put our rucksacks in a back room while we scoffed his food.

Still with eating on our minds, we toured the supermarkets and shopped until we had a small box full of groceries. This had to be carried by means of a piece of string around my neck in the manner of an old style ice-cream maid at the cinema. Then, we made for Goodwick, with the sun now shining again, hoping that nobody would try to 'stop me and buy one'.

The teacher couple appeared again, before we climbed the long hill out of Goodwick. Going out of town and seeing stretches of open grass again nearly demoralised Ruth and Joanna, and I had to keep assuring them that, if we found water, we would be able to camp on the moors at the top. Reaching the last of the houses, we saw the smoke signals of the afternoon ferry, and stood watching its progress out of the bay, across which we could see the luxury campsite of the previous night.

We should like to have camped just where we were, but of necessity, we had to go on farther. I had been tempted to knock on someone's door and ask for water, before we moved on, but couldn't face carrying it. Thus, off we went, counting the headlands off the map until we came to a small valley with a stream, marked on the map. Alas, when we got near, it proved to be too steep and overgrown to be of any use, and so it looked as if we would have to press on to Tresinwen farm, where we were sure we would be able to camp. The going here was fairly flat, and although the children were tired, they were being very good; perhaps because they were now beginning to get a bit fitter. We talked about Carregwastad Point, and how it seemed a ridiculous place at which to land to invade England, as actually happened in 1797. The whole episode was rather a pantomime, right down to the almost theatrical signing of a peace treaty in a Fishguard inn.

Before we had reached our lodging for the night, we saw some more backpackers, which are always a great stimulus to our endeavours, even when we are at home.

The contrast with the previous night's facilities was marked indeed. Now we had only a lumpy, stubbly headland of a field, and a cold-water tap, which was sited over the wall at the bottom of the field. But that brass tap shone like gold for us, with its life-sustaining fluid. Despite the fact that we couldn't see the sea, its presence was felt, nonetheless, as the flashes of Strumble Head's lighthouse spread across the countryside, picking out the tops of telegraph poles in its pulsed beam.

Our stop next day was to be at Pwll Deri Youth Hostel. This, because it was nearby, allowed us to take a more casual approach to how fast we walked, and, in fact, we walked back, to start off from the small beach where we'd left the path the previous day. We even spent a few hours paddling, watching the ferry and a group of elderly people swimming off the rocks, as well as tentatively burning our accumulated rubbish. This included the 'stop me and buy one' box along with the infinite amount of packaging that food products seem to have nowadays. In fact, apart from the bonfire, we could well have been on holiday.

A Dutch couple who we'd seen the previous afternoon, walked by, reminding us that we should be on our way, also. So, with straps made taut, we rambled on towards Strumble Head, where, along with the many visitors who were parked there, we were disappointed to find the lighthouse closed that day, in spite of the seemingly good weather, although obviously the keepers' standard of good visibility is different from ours. Regardless of this, however, we were not at all disappointed with Strumble Head itself. From its many viewpoints, it seems to hold court and reign supreme. Here, in the August sunshine, the wild flowers were beautiful, giving this rugged area an air of almost garden-like cleanliness.

There was also much to see by way of animals. In fact, I got told off for nearly treading on quite a large lizard as it darted jerkily off the sun-soaked path. We also spent a lot of time watching a seal, in a narrow cove below us. It would behave almost as it were showing off. Firstly, it would dive, twisting and turning slowly as it did so, then lazily bob to the calm, clear surface and look up at us all, for he had a fair audience by now; as if to say, "How about that, then?" It's along here that one is likely to see a peregrine falcon, but, alas, to my untrained eye, they are all kestrels, though many tell me there's no comparison.

Close to Pwll Deri there is a small, steep-sided cove, a storybook smugglers cove, with dark, sinister, sheer cliffs. Its name is Porth Maen-Melyn, which means Yellow Stone Port. This suggests that it was once a well used harbour, and accounts for the amazing set of steps carved into the rock, thus enabling cargoes to be carried up these far from yellow cliffs. At one point, the steps go behind a large cleft in the rock and come back out on the other side, and I remember staring incredulously at this powerful testimony to a previous generation's hard labour. I also wondered how on earth it was accomplished, and what others, at the time, must have thought of the one who suggested it in the first place. It was sad to see odd steps broken like the handle of some irreplaceable vase; the handrail has been twisted, bent and rusted away by winter storms, as nature claims back its property. It was also sad that this decay rendered the stairway dangerous, and so we obeyed the warning notices and reluctantly walked on by.

Ynys Melyn, or Yellow Island, from which the port must get its name, soon came into view, as did the white dot of Pwll Deri Youth Hostel. We had wondered for some time what this spot would look like, having read about Pwll Deri such things as, 'superbly situated' and 'the best situated hostel in Wales'. I must admit to a feeling of disappointment as we approached it. This was initially because, as we laboured up to the hostel, it seemed to occupy a fairly ordinary situation. Then, coming up closer and walking around to the back of the house, with its tin-sheet lean-to, I even wondered if it were the right place, but the people sitting about and waiting for it to open confirmed that we were at the right hostel. We shrugged off our misgivings and erected our home in the gorse-covered corner of a very sloping piece of ground at the back of the house, along with the Dutch couple, who shared our camping spot that night. Just when we were set up, we noticed that everyone else had gone inside the hostel, and we quickly followed suit and booked in for the night.

It was only now, as we entered the building, that the full splendour of Pwll Deri began to impinge on our senses. Walking from the office and shop area and making our way through to the main part of the hostel, we had to pass through a large, triangular conservatory, which has something of the appearance of a sculptor's studio. The walls are covered in display cabinets, which are full of antique bottles and the skulls of seabirds, the latter being appropriate to the area. The most outstanding aspect, however, was the side that formed the hypotenuse of this amazing room; it is a single, full-length window, which looks right down the series of high cliffs that border the coast to Carnllidi and St David's. If that isn't good enough to please, one can go out to the veranda beyond, drink in the view neat, and grow inebriated in its beauty. However, slotting that into our mental pending file, and in almost hungry panic, we were more intent on finding out what facilities were available at this, our second hostel.

Some visitors were a little surprised at how quickly we had the table laid in the room with a view, and were sat, eating bacon grill, beans and mashed potato, followed by peaches and custard. Our alacrity was due to us being used to preparing the same meal under more adverse conditions, and we had a hidden agenda, too. We wanted to get the best seats in the house. Oh, and we cheated by buying the peaches from the hostel shop. We sat there with our pots of tea, lording it over all we surveyed, and declaring ourselves very fortunate indeed. We wondered how much it would have cost us to have eaten a meal in such surroundings, had we been staying at a suitable hotel.

We certainly didn't take that meal for granted, although it's strange how we all often do just that. We turn the tap, flush the loo, stuff the dustbin, and give no thought to whence it came, or whither it goes. This fact was brought home to us all that evening, when the water supply simply ran out. Many appeals were made by campers to the warden, everyone expecting that a phone-call to the local council, or the turn of some valve, would set matters right again. The warden soberly told the complainants that they'd used up their ration too quickly, and lost the pressure in the long water pipe that stretched between here and the main supply pipe. Everyone was very good about it, although the evening was punctuated by periods of sudden cheers and subsequent runs to the kitchen sink, which was very full of dishes, every time the tap ran for a few seconds and then stopped.

The girls managed to have a wash, although I had to wait for mine until gone ten o'clock. Even so, the evening can only be described as enchanting. The sea, after the sun had set, began to look like a sheet of ice. It was then that I realized how deceptive the heights were, and that this, truthfully, was quite a place, 'superbly positioned', and possibly, 'the best in Wales'. I had certainly underestimated Pwll Deri, when we'd first arrived. It was dark when we reluctantly retired, and the dew could be sensed in the chill of the night air. After an evening of Deri dominoes and Deri drought, it was Deri dew.

The Deri dawn came for us at seven o'clock, and although we waited for the warden to give us a job to do, none came our way. Before we left, we made a point of savouring the last of the hostel's comforts, which included a much larger breakfast than usual. We had porridge, followed by scrambled egg on toast, which we ate at a fine table, laid with knives and forks. We cleared the tables and did some tidying up, and still got away by half past ten, which was a lot earlier than we had expected.

We had a fair way to go that day, if we were to arrive at Trefin. Starting at stile number 343, we had already clocked 135 stiles since Sunday, and it was now Saturday. It should have acted as a warning, as became apparent to us later in the day.

From Pwll Deri, the walking in any direction must be good. With the height gained in getting there, the rewards come in the form of grand vistas. In fact, if you can find the time, a steep walk up to Garn Fawr, which is almost behind the hostel, is more than worth the effort. In the first place, it is the site of one of the finest stone forts in Britain, and that is despite the contribution its stones have made to local wall-building. However, it was the outstanding panoramic view that struck us. Apart from its obvious scenic value, the view was also one with real meaning for us because we could pick out places we knew, right down the coast to Skomer Island, and so we pointed to them and exclaimed, in high excitement.

Chapter 8

The path and view to Trefin was no exception to the local beauty. The path to Abermawr could be clearly seen in the distance, but in the foreground, it was a bit vague, as it followed the ridge beyond the hostel. Though comparatively low in altitude and so near the sea, the area has a mountainous feel to it. We were tempted to go down to the sandy cove of Pwll Crochan and join the couple of families there, but I persuaded Ruth and, particularly, Joanna, to walk on to Aber Mawr, knowing that it was a reasonable way to Trevin. Passing across the crowded beach of Aber Bach, I still didn't relate the crowd to the fact that it was Saturday. We continued on to Aber Mawr, where we had our beach lunch. In spite of being down to sea level at this, the old transatlantic cable terminus, the area still had that mountain feel to it, and we had what I consider a mountain-walkers' lunch of brown bread with sardines and tomato. Tinned fish, if you can manage to carry it, is good, cheap protein. It reminds me of reading about one stout fellow who walked the length of the Alps. Along the way he sang the praises of his little tins of fish, which seemed to be his staple diet. This was his food, even when he was going through trendy, expensive Swiss resorts.

We sat and watched people enjoying the seaside. One little chap had even taken his bike with him, much to the amusement of us all. His performance worked up to a climax as his circuit of the water's edge took him deeper and deeper into the surf, until he was finally forced to jump off and wheel his cycle out, its wheels looking like grotesque spiders' webs, as the whole machine was draped in seaweed. Nonetheless, after clearing this away from around the chain, he rode around on his uniquely decorated bicycle with youthful nonchalance.

On the beach, which was quite crowded, by Pembrokeshire standards, we spotted three girls who had also shared with us the comforts of Pwll Deri. One of these, as she'd told us the previous day, while waiting for the hostel to open, was walking the path and using the hostel as her base. Seeing the girls move on was our cue to do likewise, with a little persuasion for my girls. The path soon became overgrown with very tall ferns, and halfway through them, we met the one girl going back to her beloved base. She assured us that this type of overgrown terrain didn't go on forever, although we were beginning to have our doubts. When we did eventually get out onto the open headland, the jungle was soon forgotten, especially when we came down into the crowded area of Abercastle, with all its boats and dinghies and consequent colour and activity. Although the Abercastle detour inland was reminiscent of Solva's meandering way, we sensed the difference here, where the coast provides reminders of the past industrial misuse. Nonetheless, the beauty has returned, to be enjoyed by a generation that appears to be better in some respects than previous generations, but, sadly, not in all its ways.

We filled our water bottles from taps in the toilets, we started to walk out of Abercastle, because the path goes back out towards the sea, and it was hereabouts that my concern had been concentrated for some time. This was due to various warnings about the sheer cliffs, and the path being liable to subsidence. It was exactly as I had feared: the path ran consistently near the edge of the cliff and there was almost no grass verge or any other sort of growth to soften the rugged, vertical view, and the subsidence was no mere crumble affair. One whole section, about two hundred yards in length, had just dropped about fifteen feet. One walks cautiously around this natural amphitheatre, wanting to hurry, but afraid to do so, lest one should trip or stumble. The problem here was not so much the up and down as the in and out, and it seemed a long detour from Pwllong to Trefin beach. The path makes almost a full circle of the village, which was our real objective.

It was during this frustrating exercise that the reality of our situation hit home. It was Saturday afternoon. The shops, if there were any, would soon be shut, and we were nearly out of food, except for some dehydrated food and porridge oats. We also had very little cash, and in these pre-cash-dispenser days, the Post Office, if there were one, would certainly be closed. Therefore, the long way round seemed to be that much longer, and was concluded by a walk uphill on the road from the beach. I must say everyone was very good about it; perhaps it was the thought of actually sleeping in a bed that night. Joanna was certainly thrilled at the idea, and dying to see the actual building, which, as we had repeatedly told her, was an old school. I can't imagine what picture that must have prompted in her young mind.

One of the first buildings we found was the Post Office, although, apart from the sign outside, you'd never know what it was because it looked like an ordinary, modern bungalow. The front door was open and we wondered if, by any chance, it was open. Just through the front door, in what must have been a passage, was the hatch that had been installed when the building was converted into a post office. The office was closed, but the resident postmistress very kindly let us draw out some money. After this little boost to our confidence, we had a short walk up the village, past the closed shop, to the school that was to be our lodging for the night.

By youth hostel standards, Poppit Sands and Pwll Deri had been listed as standard, but Trefin was graded simple, not that there were any fewer comforts, but the individuality of hostels is truly amazing, regardless of the standard set by their organizing body. We walked into the large hall, which was humming with activity. This one room had every thing in it that we could require, except the beds. The office was contained within the warden's handbag, which reposed in a drawer of one the many kitchen tables. With boots and rucksacks, and no tent to put them into, we all felt a bit awkward. We were soon led away, I to the men's dormitory, and the girls to the women's one, after we had made hasty arrangements to meet later. The warden proved to be very good to us indeed. While preparing the tea, I noticed a boy with a fresh loaf of bread, and I asked him where he'd managed to obtain it, expecting him to describe some distant or closed shop.

"From the warden," he replied.

"Have you another?" I asked the warden.

She had another and it made quite a difference to our food shortage problem, which was compounded by the fact that the next day was Sunday and there would be no shops open. We settled down to a good meal, after which Judith spoke to the other two girls who had been on Abermawr beach at lunchtime. One of them was Australian and full of praise for the coast path. It often takes a stranger to appreciate the beauty we have around us, or on our doorstep, and take for granted.

★ ★ ★

This reminded me of when Judith and I were in Snowdonia, on our honeymoon, I remember us getting a lift from a salesman who was passing through Capel Curig, on his way to Caernarfon. He said that he was unsure of the way and would be glad of our company, to navigate for him. Coming out of Capel Curig and past the twin lakes of Llynau Mymbyr, I was able to point out Snowdon and explain that that it was our proposed destination. He exclaimed at how good the view was, and explained that, from studying his motorist map, he had not realised that the country was going to be like this. He was a sales representative, who had a name on a form, and an address highlighted in red.

After we had turned right past Pen-y-Gwryd and were climbing the winding road to Pen-y-Pass, he started to become quite enthusiastic about the views, explaining that he'd just spent a great deal of money on a visit to Switzerland, completely unaware that this was just on his doorstep, as it were. At Trefin, a young Australian girl, who had travelled halfway round the World, was enjoying something that many British, even Welsh people, have never seen, or are ever likely to see properly, unless they get out and walk a little.

★ ★ ★

Meanwhile, our friend the warden sidled up to me and furtively explained something about our sleeping arrangement, which she did not, apparently, want to be overheard. She told me that a family had made a booking over the phone, and if they turned up she would have to open the extra dormitory, which was outside, across the playground, but if they failed to appear, and that seemed likely by this time, we could have the dormitory to ourselves, so that we could stay together as a family. This was quite something to think about, and we sat on pins for the rest of the evening, watching for any new arrivals, the children even more tense than us. Eventually, we followed the warden, who jingled a large bundle of keys, and were ushered into a plain, little building, which held only four bunk beds and a washbasin. Nonetheless, it made a beautiful little home for us privileged four. Joanna, especially, liked the idea of Dad not being on his own, but, more importantly she could sleep in one of those lovely little beds she had spoken of so often. Ruth, being that bit older, appreciated what the warden had done, and still had a latent fear that this mysterious family could still arrive and steal our newly found home. However, they didn't show up, and we retained our private suite. With the sunset shining through the open door, we decided that someone was on our side again.

At about 7.30 on the following morning we were awoken by the sound of flushing toilets. They all stood in a row outside, exposed to the cool morning air, as school toilets used to be. A simple, wholesome breakfast of porridge and toast set us up for yet another day on our feet. Once again, the warden had apparently failed to find us a job to do, but we tidied up and brushed the carpet as well as we could, endeavouring, in true boy-scout fashion, to leave the place tidier than we had found it. Just as we walked across the playground, about to go through the hostel and away, the warden came out and said that that she'd forgotten about us and had nearly locked us in, which would have been an unusual experience, and was, perhaps, why we weren't assigned a chore.

It was a bit of a grey day, and once we were back on the path, the sea mist was thick and we could barely see the waves at the foot of the cliffs below us. Then, as the day brightened, the dark areas slowly became visible as rocks and cliffs, and we could see the waves clearly. Finally, the mist crept slowly out to sea and disappeared. Much to the joy of Ruth and Joanna, the only food available at Porthgain was sweets and ice cream, which I must admit to enjoying, as well.

The walk back out of this place, which was yet another industrial museum, conjured up thoughts of what an extremely busy place it must have been in its heyday. It is gradually becoming busy again now, making its money from tourism, as more and more people discover the pleasures of quiet, out of the way places like this. I think the Sloop Inn is possibly the initial magnet.

The long flight of steps out of the harbour brought us suddenly into a type of wilderness, the ground having been sifted by quarrymen; in fact, we mistook a quarry road for the path and ended up in the quarry, with no way out except by scaling its sides. Nonetheless, beauty was never very far away and, even here, we saw another small butterfly, which we had, by now, proudly come to know as the Small British Blue, a name which always amuses me; I think of it as the ultimate patriotic title. It is an incident like this that illustrates how walking and climbing bring you into close contact with the natural world. No matter how slow you are to learn, if you take the trouble to look them up in reference books, it is inevitable that you will become familiar with the names of various birds, plants and animals. The build-up of knowledge comes slowly at first, perhaps, but when it is enhanced by the study of history, geography, geology and meteorology, a full appreciation of what there is in the great outdoors becomes possible. Meteorology is an almost universal subject of conversation, no matter what level one reaches in the study of this, the elusive science.

We successfully clambered out of the quarry and found the path again. This brought us to Traeth Llyfn; on the way there we came across a few small places called Porth Something, although it is not possible today to see quite how they acquired their appellation, since there is no longer any sign of them having been used as ports or harbours.

Traeth Llyfn is an idyllic place, and its name, meaning Sleek Shore or Beach, is very fitting. In spite of it being off the beaten tourist track, it was far from empty of visitors. We debated whether the walk back up to the path, which we had left in order to reach the beach, but we decided to see what Abereiddy had to offer, as our arrival there would coincide with our normal lunch-time, and fit well into our schedule. There was also the chance that there would be an open shop there. However, it had nothing more than an ice-cream van, and so we were reduced to dining on bread and water, having run out of reconstituted fruit juice.

Judith and I sat on the wall at the top of the beach, looking like a pair of pensioners, while the two girls went for a paddle. In spite of the beach seeming to be popular, it was a bit disappointing. The sands are very dark, almost black, resulting in a muddy mess, which seems to delight the children and horrify all the mothers.

The history of Abereiddy is somewhat sad. Slate-quarrying started here, in competition with the quarries in Caernarvonshire, but the quarry owners never enjoyed the success of their northern brothers. The industry resulted in the formation of strange areas of coastline to the north of the beach. One of these is called The Blue Lagoon, and, seeing it at low tide, I was mystified as to how the boats got in there. The answer is that, at high tide, the sea enters a channel carved through the almost coal-black rock. However, the butterflies abounded, and we saw grey and brown ones with orange wingtips, as well as some white ones, which seemed to have a lime green flash. We saw also funnel-shaped webs, leading down into the ground, where, no doubt, the spider host awaited its next unwitting guest. Before we moved on again, we filled our water bottles.

Somewhere around here, the coastline started to regain the grandeur of Pwll Deri and Strumble Head, as the path slowly gained height, in order to cross Penberry. However, it was already late afternoon, and we were hoping to see a campsite or farm, or, failing either of these, even a patch of grass and a stream. We had noticed a lone back-packer behind us, who caught us up as we reached Penberry, where we shared the great views back towards Pwll Deri and Strumble Head and forward to St David's Head. The height at this point makes it hard to believe that one is still on the coast path. He and I were busy with our cameras, trying to take away a little of the marvel of it all on film. He told us that he had left Fishguard at 6 o'clock that morning, and walked a distance that had taken us nearly three days. I reflected on days when I had walked alone, and how I had felt the urge to drive myself that bit further, walking faster and taking fewer rest breaks. I cannot explain this, unless it is due to an instinct to find company, but it's certainly true that, when walking in mountainous terrain, one has to be careful not to exhaust oneself, which, under some circumstances, could prove disastrous.

As our lone walker shot off to St David's, his new rucksack on his back, we turned inland, in the hope that an orange mist that we could see in the distance would materialize into a campsite, which it did, and a very good one it was. We tried to purchase food at the farm, but all they could provide were milk and eggs, but with our good supply of dehydrated foods, we enjoyed a generous helping of Soya TVP with beef stock on rice, and oceans of tea. This was closely followed by sessions of revelling in hot water; first it was to wash the dishes, then, the laundry, and finally, the serious joy of the Portacabin shower. All around us was the usual assortment of holidaymakers. There was an exception to what I describe as the usual, because the family next door to us had brought their unusual pets, one of which made me jump in amazement. It was a beautiful falcon.

We spent a pleasant evening playing cards, talking about how best to arrange what would be our last walking day; a week had passed since our rest day at Newport. The next day, however, exposed a reluctance to rush. While we slowly packed, our neighbours on the other side showed extreme interest in what we were doing. I thought it might be due to their almost obsessive interest in keeping fit that they thought that backpacking would be just the thing for them. I didn't ask them, but I wondered. There's so much more to backpacking than being fit in body, it is quite different from normal camping holidays.

I calculated that, when we reached Whitesands Bay that day, we would have completed over one hundred and thirty miles of the coast path, each mile full of delights and things to remember with pleasure. I wondered where the time had gone. It was midday before we finally reached the path again, on the map it was no more than a dotted line. It skirted fields and, at one stage, we ended up the wrong side of an electric fence, and it took an awful lot of persuasion to get Joanna to crawl underneath it. The irony is that it probably wasn't even switched on. The last part of this path took us near to Ffos-y-Mynach, meaning Ditch of the Monk, which was a reminder that we were getting near to St David's, a place of many ecclesiastical legends and ancient superstitions. The view of the aforementioned St. David's Head was there to greet us, just as we had left it yesterday, and the heathers gave the scene a park-like quality, the purple colour backed by varying shades of green, and the sea.

It was late in the morning before we got going on Ffos-y-Cefnpwnwr and we had not travelled far before the call for lunch rang out loud and clear. We found a suitable length of rock slab and a good view, rationed out our last cream crackers and cake, and, having so little of it, we talked about food. Our hope was that the beach shop at Porth Mawr or Whitesands would sell some of the things that were on the list we recited, which consisted of all the things we would like to eat and drink just then.

From our vantage point, we were able to view Pwll Deri and just beyond it, we saw the flash of Strumble Head lighthouse. We watched the distant light and reflected on how much lay between there and here. Many were our memories of the many beauties seen and appreciated, all of them having been brought before our eyes by our humble feet. Beyond our present horizon lay yet more gems, stretching right back to Poppitt Sands. Although we felt like some old explorers, on our meagre rations, we also felt like some sort of pioneers, breaking into territory that was fresh and virgin, at least, that is how it appeared to us, as each panoramic page was turned.

Nonetheless, all good things come to an end, and so we had to re-pack our sacks, swing them, expertly now, onto our backs, and stretch our much fitter legs. Those fit legs enjoyed the pleasantness of the path and its absence of ups and downs, although there were many fine ups and downs all around us, including Carn Ludi, a regular Matterhorn, and yet of embarrassingly low altitude. I hadn't looked closely at the map of this part of the route, thinking it was just a matter of going around the point to Porth Mawr, where we had travelled before. Hence, the good expanse of sand at Porthmelgan came as a very pleasant surprise. It was, however, a bit of a pull up from here, and we also had the unusual experience of having a cat follow us; a dog we could understand, but, somehow, the cat, which was almost a kitten, just didn't fit any theories we could offer at the time. Finally, while it was amusing itself in one of its playful interludes in the grass, we managed to steal away.

With the path now narrowing…

With the path now narrowing, along with the extra people who were in this relatively popular area, we had many a hold-up, but the nods, apologies, smiles and thanks made it very different from the wheeled variety of traffic hold-up. The car park, which seemed to be a hot, smelly kind of spot, as we walked self-consciously across it, was lined with cars. We were hoping that the shop sold more than the usual buckets, spades, postcards and ice cream. Much to our surprise and delight, they seemed to sell just about all the food that we had longed for, and we all filled our arms with good things, and decided which we could carry further and which we could eat now. 'Now' is the correct word, for we sat right outside the shop and savoured the gleanings from this emporium of delights. However, there was also the added pleasure of not having to save a bit until later. After satisfyingly brushing the crumbs away, screwing up and depositing the packaging debris, we trudged wearily on to Rhosson, where we'd stayed previously, when we were on another visit to this stretch of our Pembroke Coast walk. I say that we trudged, because a lot of the path here is very sandy and this makes it hard going, even though the going is soft. Our plans had been to camp at a site near the small beach below Rhosson, but this site sloped a lot and the people who were staying there looked a bit rowdy, which would have been in sharp contrast to that to which we were becoming accustomed, which is why we opted for a longer walk and a known campsite.

The tents were soon up and we began to revive memories of our previous visit, but we felt so much older now, not so much in years, but in experience and appreciation. We thought about the number of stiles we'd crossed, having started that morning at number 286 and finished at 281. This amounted to a meagre five, but, from the start at Poppit Sands, we'd crossed a total of 197, which seemed a lot to accomplish in just seven days walking, and remembering our day off at Newport. Therefore, while we had only crossed five today, it was forty-five on the day we walked to Newport, and on some days it had been over thirty. It seemed to us to be proof of our growing experience and improved fitness.

Once again, with this being a holiday area, people started to take notice of us. Our tents are smaller than theirs, sometimes they appear peculiar, and, unlike most of our fellow campers, we had no car. This is what other people find most peculiar about us; we are seen to arrive in an out of the way place, free of this luxury, which, for many, has become a necessity, like so many other things that we can actually manage without if we want to.

Nonetheless, here we were, with no apparent means of transport other than our feet.

People stop us and ask, "Have you been walking the coast path?"

I wonder how they knew. However, to be fair, the couple who spoke to us on this occasion was quite serious, and keen to talk to us about our travels. They, like so many others, loved walking, and their children didn't. Like so many children today, theirs wanted the bright lights, which means, in part, an eternal jangle in the pocket and jingle in the ear, and a jungle in which to do it. At least, that's how the parents see it, once the cord of communication is broken. The father seemed very interested in our equipment, due partly to his being employed by a company producing nylon fibre products. I could sympathise with him, and could remember when I also looked longingly at others doing so much in North Wales and envying them but unable to do anything about it because of the children. Now, I marvelled at how blessed we were, having children who, if we were reasonable with them, reward us with more than fine times together. Our hesitant decisions taken in earlier days had proved to be right, so far, but, more importantly, right for us. In the way that there's more to backpacking than being fit, there's more to family backpacking than just taking the kids along. There has to be quite a close, day-to-day life-style, and this bridges the generation gap, but how that is achieved is another story.

The next day, we were back to the realities of everyday life, and I had to go back to fetch the car; it took three buses and a few miles of walking. With that and the reminiscing as I travelled along,

I realized that we had covered quite a respectable distance. Walking up the lane from Poppit Sands, I almost felt as if I could start all over again, only with a little more confidence this time, due to knowing what was around the corner. After walking for so long, and then struggling all day with buses, it seemed unbelievable that this plush machine of mine, this car complete with air conditioning and stereo, was ready to propel me wherever I chose to go. However, necessity made the choice for me; that was, supermarket shopping in Fishguard, to buy food for my starving family, at home in the campsite. I arrived back there in time for tea, having left at eight that morning. Needless to say, we had a scrumptious meal, gorged ourselves uncomfortable, and revelled in something that had obsessed us for days: fresh grapefruit.

The rest of the holiday was mostly spent on beaches, and in visits to favourite little haunts, but the next highlight was a boat trip around Ramsey Isle. We felt that to go around this southern extremity would complete the trip around the coastline.

We arrived at the lifeboat station just as a party was returning, which meant that we now had to wait until enough people had gathered to warrant a trip out. A mist came up off the sea, and many people left, due no doubt, to nerves, but I'm pleased to say that just a handful of us did eventually go, and it was well worth the long wait. The boat owner's vast experience became very apparent as he picked his way through the currents, which could be felt as they took hold of the boat, and its engine throttle was opened up, to resist them. Around the far side of the island, the swell was greater, though the pull of current seemed to be less. The skipper quite nonchalantly walked down the boat as it chugged along, unmanned, quite close to cliffs and rocks. He appeared to get back, unhurriedly, just in time to adjust the steering. Then, we quietly slunk in and out of a maze of rocks and pinnacles, to see the profusion of seals for which Ramsey is so famous. It was, indeed, a fine finale to this part of our Pembrokeshire plod. Perhaps, if we'd planned it differently, we could have had the day on the island itself, and walked around its cliff tops, but, as it was, we were more than pleased.

Chapter 9

I changed my job and we moved house during the following year, which meant that we had to miss our walk on the coast path but we had some enjoyable walks along the abandoned railway tracks of Derbyshire, which would, I am sure, prove to be a great source of nostalgia to even the least enthusiastic of railway enthusiasts. Although, in some ways, these walks provide attractions similar to those of Pembrokeshire, to summarise them in terms of flora and fauna is rather a cold way to catalogue them. It is true that the arrival and expansion of the motorway has brought back the kestrel; likewise, the disused railways have grown wild grasses and plants, which, in turn, attract many rare butterflies. This is because some of these depend on particular grasses, which cannot survive on normal farming land, due to annual ploughing and seeding. Thus, the old railways have become an unexpected source of nature reserves, as well as providing the public with recreational paths and parks. Many local authorities have taken advantage of these strips of land, and used them to clean up an area and create a park. The abandoned railway track is fast becoming the long distance path of the future. In this generation, which has seen a manic speeding-up of everything, the railway joins the old pilgrim ways, Roman roads and medieval, green lanes. They have become an old way, and the generation that remembers the clunk of the carriage door, the echoed calls, waves and whistles that heralded the immortal steam train is a dying breed.

Eventually, the time came when we sat down and began to

plan our final assault on the coast path. We had been fussy in the past about where we would walk, and we were now left with that awkward part around Milford Haven, which goes from Mullock Bridge around to Pembroke, and from there, around to Freshwater East, leaving the better half until last. It was a stretch of path that would present several problems. Apart from the campsites at either end, I only knew for certain of one other site, which was at Angle, and a possible site at Sandy Haven. Another problem, and not a small one, was where to leave our car. This section is so diverse, and the buses were not convenient, should we need to use them, especially at the Dale end. If only we'd walked nearer Milford on the previous occasion, it would have made quite a difference, but it was no good crying over spilt milk.

It was decided eventually to leave supplies of water at a series of places between Pembroke and Freshwater East, and do the top bit as day walks from Herbrandston, assuming there was a site there. Even as we shopped in Pembroke, the final decisions hadn't been made with any conviction; but I did decide that it would be best to get the awkward and, perhaps, not so scenic Milford section done first. It's a shame, to be talking of this National Park as something to got done and out of the way. Nonetheless, that's how it appeared at the time, while we desperately sought to find a solution. I couldn't face studying bus timetables any longer, and so we just drove over the bridge to Herbrandston, to check at the farm about camping. Unbelievably, there didn't seem to be a proper campsite there, just a few people camping at the far end of what really is the car park. It seemed as if there was no end to this problem?

Now, it was a matter of getting on to Mullock Bridge, getting started and worrying about the car later. The Oasis was still there, and it seemed little changed and the woman that ran it before was still there. However, the house extension, which was in progress when we visited it before, was now completed, and we camped in a different field. We sorted out all our gear, and tried to sleep as if we were without the car, so that we would be ready for the morning, and could set off with the minimum of preparation.

Here we were again at Dale, which seemed to feature so much in our walking of the coast. It had been our goal on the first trip, and here it was again, now at the start of this section. It's a little place, and yet has many claims to fame; one being that it was from here that Nicolette Milnes set sail on the 12th June 1971, in a 30-foot sloop, and forty-five days later, she arrived in America; the first woman to sail single-handed across the Atlantic. Another event, of much greater significance, happened a lot longer ago, on 7th August 1485, to be precise. It was almost 500 years to the day, when Henry Tudor, a small group of Lancastrian exiles and a force of French mercenaries, numbering some 2,000 in all, landed at Dale. Fifteen days later, the armies of Tudor and the King met at a place now known as Bosworth Field. The result was total victory for Henry Tudor and his cause, the destruction of the last of the Plantagenet houses and the House of York, and the birth of a new dynasty, the Tudors. What happened between August 7th and 22nd is equally fascinating and laudable. A small force of exiles and mercenaries, incredibly, chose to challenge the might and power of the English Crown. This small army marched at almost unbelievable speed over the rough and rugged terrain of West and mid Wales, gathering support and recruits as it went, and ever fearful of the task that lay before it. It was proclaimed by the bards of Wales that Henry Tudor was the *Mab Darogan* (Son of Prophecy). At last, a Welshman had come to claim what was considered his birthright, the throne of England. At the head of his army, the Red Dragon

Standard was raised, the legendary symbol of the great Welsh chieftain, Cadwallader, although it is also an apocalyptic symbol of someone else.

We wondered where our life had gone in the time since we were last here; our musings prompted by the curlew's echoed call from the nearby estuary. It was as if this little corner of creation had stood still since we were last here, and we might have been listening to the same bird that had charmed us many months ago.

The following morning was very misty and there seemed to be no sign of it clearing when we moved off at quarter to twelve. Although it was a late start, it didn't matter too much, as it was not very far to Sandy Haven. We left the road at Lower Mullock Farm and our path proved to be very overgrown, and it took us quite some time to tread down the fog-drenched nettles. We eventually came out into a field, the path now being non-existent, and we walked through the grass and stray corn on the side of the field. Our legs and boots were soon soaked, which set us to wondering how much more of our chosen path would be overgrown to the same degree. After walking along another field, where the hay lay flat because of the rain that had fallen in the past months, it came as a great relief to emerge onto a lane, which led down to the salt waters of the estuary. It was high tide and it looked good, in spite of the mist, which showed signs of lifting. There was a profusion of honeysuckle on one side of us and flotsam and jetsam on the other, although, strictly speaking, it was probably just plain rubbish.

At the point where the causeway can be crossed at low water, we looked for suitable stones, and sat down to lunch, while nervously wondering whether it would rain. For entertainment we had water-skiing quite close by, and what we supposed to be a very proficient sportsman proved to be a sportswoman. This became apparent when she stopped and we heard across the water her clear voice in conversation with someone. She handed her skis and wet-suit over to a man. Now the real entertainment was to start. He had obviously never water-skied before. This became very apparent as we listened to the girl's brief instructions and the man's amusing comments, and his antics when he tried to put on the skis while in the water.

Then came the moment for which we had all been waiting. With the tips of his skis poking untidily just out of the water, the boat engine picked up speed, causing the man to dive forward in the water, with no sign of lift at all. This set us all off into uncontrollable giggles, led by Joanna, who had to be reminded to control herself, for fear our voices would be heard over the water, with its sound-carrying effect. Now began a hilarious series of lessons, dives and yells, and it became obvious that he must have been a bit of a comic in his normal life. When eventually he managed to straighten his legs and stand up, he let out a triumphant Yippee, only to cartwheel straight back into the water. On the next try, though, he'd got the hang of it, and did a lap of honour, only to crash land when he tried to wave. However, for the following effort, the boat speeded up, and the whole performance carried on for some time. This gave me the impression that he was like the proverbial man holding on to the tiger's tail, too weary to carry on and too much in fear to let go. Then, when he crossed the wake of the boat, his plight and our free entertainment ended.

Presently, we walked further along the beach and saw some children in life jackets. They would cast off and row their dinghy close to the shore, as they quietly enjoyed the simple pleasure of being afloat.

We cut through a small farmyard and emerged onto the coast

path proper, passing en route a county council van. The reason for the presence the van became evident when we found ourselves walking along a freshly trimmed path and heard the sound of distant strimmers. It was satisfying to speculate on how thickly the grass on the path must have been, and to imagine that it had been cut just in time for us to walk over it in comfort. It was also satisfying to know that the council was considerate enough to undertake the upkeep of these less popular parts of the path. However, what do you do when you're walking behind a council worker who's using a motor strimmer and wearing earmuffs? You want to get by, and he can't hear you, and so, you just have to follow him patiently, in the hope that he will see you through the corner of his goggled eye. It will happen, but it's just a question of when.

Our first good view came when we arrived at the archway to Monk Haven. The latter framed the former, and the centre of our interest and of the picture was a small tanker, which was anchored just offshore. We would see many more during the course of this holiday, as they waited for their respective berths within the haven. Had the beach been deserted, we probably would have stopped for a while, but we went on towards Watch House Point. It's a very apt title, in view of the many deserted lookouts and gun mountings, along with what I presumed were some sort of armouries. Many of them were half hidden in the bracken, and some were being utilized for storing hay, like the coastguard's look-out at Cemaes Head. By the time we'd got around to Lindsway Bay, we began to feel like taking a rest. This was prompted by the fact that there was a bench, where we sat, soaking up the sun and admiring views of sea and countryside. We were able to see down the peninsula as far as Great Castle Head. It was a very satisfying place to be, on a satisfying day, and we could well imagine it to be a secret haunt for many of St Ishmael's villagers.

It was now that we began to feel the effects of our first day back on the road. The rucksacks were being held that few seconds longer, before being hefted onto the first shoulder, bearing in mind that these were no mere shopping bags. Once we had started to move again, I noticed the Coastguard's Land Rover up on the ridge that leads down to Great Castle Head. As we got nearer, the man himself could be seen, with his binoculars aimed in our direction. When we were nearer still, I tried to get into conversation with the man. I admit to a certain curiosity about this. He was a very amiable sort of a chap, and told us how a container containing toxic substances had been washed up, and it was now leaking into a plastic bag in the Land Rover. We presumed he was looking out to see if any more were being washed up. Some time later, other vehicles arrived, joined the coastguard, and they all drove off together.

The path was a bit overgrown around Great Castle Head, then, we were provided with a pleasant interlude in the form of a pair of girls riding on a special trailer behind a tractor. They sat in what looked like very comfortable seats, then, taking small cabbage plants, at least, that is what they looked like, they placed them in a funnel, from which they ended up mechanically planted in the warm Pembrokeshire soil. The whole contraption was covered over, and clanked its way across a vast field. A meander through a short stretch of woodland brought us down into Sandy Haven, where we were pleased to find that the tide was out, thus enabling us to cross the little causeway there. A group of exited boys were catching crabs, in fact, catching doesn't seem to be the right word for what they were doing. They were lifting them out of the water, one after the other, to various accompanying shouts and exited gasps of horror.

After we had crossed the water and made our way up the lane to our campsite, we soon set up our camp and enjoyed our first dehydrated meal on this stretch of coast. After this relaxed and relaxing meal, we savoured the warm evening of a warm day, down by the now deserted causeway.

There were plenty of crabs, but we had no way of catching them, and we couldn't stop, anyway, because the tide was beginning to rise. This was quite a sight to behold. This being an estuary, in the haven itself there is barely a ripple, and you can watch the tide creep relentlessly over the sand.

Apart from the tide factor, there was the time factor, we were soon in bed, after a first day that had seemed longer than, in fact, it was. We were disturbed briefly during the night by some party-boppers; we assumed they had come to see the sea. This was a bit irritating because I had to be up at 5.45 on the following morning, go back by road, fetch the car and take it to this side of Milford Haven, so that we could cheat and drive, rather than walk, through Milford Haven. I had to cross the causeway before the tide rose to cover it, if I were to avoid making the long inland detour.

All was quiet and the air was fresh and invigorating, as I pattered along the lanes that morning. The wildlife I saw made no sound: a motionless heron in the estuary, a rabbit, big enough to have been a hare, on the edge of a field. As I came out of the wooded valley that leads up from Sandy Haven, the land levelled out and the increasing daylight revealed distant, fertile fields. The lane ran straight and boasted a line of telegraph poles. A yellowhammer flew ahead of me, moving from pole to pole, giving its unique call that is supposed to sound like 'a little bit of bread and no cheese', although I heard it as, 'I can keep in front of you-oo', as it kept three poles ahead of me.

I felt a smug contentedness at having the world to myself. At the end of the lane was the turn off to St Ishmael, and as I was about to take it, I was startled to be addressed by a stranger. She said, "Hello." I saw a woman, who was sitting at a gate near the junction. She was smiling and holding a note pad. I told her that I hadn't expected to see anyone this early; she said that neither had she.

The morning spell was now broken, and, soon after this encounter, I passed a group of boys cheerily ambling along, and life seemed relatively normal again. All was quiet and still as I walked through St Ishmael, where the only sign of life I saw was a man creeping out of his house, getting into his car, probably about to drive to his work. I crept out of village, climbed into my car and took a much needed rest before driving to our appointed rendezvous.

I found an excellent shop on the outskirts of Milford Haven and had to discipline myself not to buy too much, knowing that I would have to carry it, but in no time at all, I was back with the girls. We spent a hot day on the beach, where we were already ensconced comfortably by twenty past ten, much to the astonishment of some of the other campers. By two o'clock, having had lunch on the beach, it was getting too hot for comfort, and we went back to the tents. The long walk and the very hot sun had made me feel a bit dizzy, and I spent the rest of baking hot afternoon sprawled out in the tent, which we had kept relatively cool by draping our sleeping bags over the top.

When backpacking in very hot weather, the full meaning of the words: 'the relentless sun', becomes self evident, and the first thing a man wants in a parched land is not cool water but cool shade. It was our good fortune to have chosen this day as a day off. After our first day away from home comforts, it had given us an excellent day on a relatively quiet beach. It also rescued us from walking a good distance on a scorching hot day. I recalled a time when we were walking through Abercastle, and Judith telling us that her legs were frying, and she longed for quiet, level stretches of path, where she could drape towels over them as she walked.

At this time of year, July, the potato crop is harvested, and the transporters manage to shed some of their load. We were walking along lanes that were littered with potatoes. I couldn't resist picking up enough for us to have for tea, along with dried vegetables and tinned sardines. Once more I was reminded of that determined chap who walked the length of the Alps alone, and sang the praises of 'the little tins of fish'; his main source of food.

A woman with some sort of camper van camped next to us. She had planned to prepare a more exotic meal for herself, and had been looking forward to it all afternoon, which she had spent windsurfing. We were curious observers, prepared to sniff the cooking aromas and admire her culinary skills. She started to prepare the meal, but suddenly, she began to pack everything away into her mobile home. She started the engine and drove away, yelling something about finding gas. We shook our heads. It was well past the time when all the local shops closed for the day.

After a long time, she returned with a bottle of gas, and when she went to attach it to her cooker, she discovered that the thread was damaged. Then, to top it all, she was sure that it had been the last gas bottle in the shop. Our starving girl jumped back into her vehicle, her stomach, no doubt, rumbling noisily.

Meanwhile, we all went down to the causeway and watched the little crabs that are to be found in abundance around the little bridge there. Using cockles as bait, I fished out our first crab, by means of a simple line and stick. After initial exclamations of horror and fear, the girls became curious, and were soon lifting out crabs themselves, and watching them plop back in, seemingly unaware of their proximity to the edge of the causeway. Whilst we were engrossed in this, along came a small boy, accompanied by his older sister, May. We got to know her name because everything the boy said seemed to have the prefix May, as he excitedly pointed at crabs in the water or on the end of our line. He then tried hopefully to hook one out, using some string, and so we kitted him out with half of a cockle, and laughed as his excitement reached fever pitch. Soon, it was time to persuade the girls to leave May and her brother, and we gathered up our pile of cockles, but no crabs, and made our way back to our tents.

Stiles had come to have significance for us, much as the old fashioned milestones must have had for travellers in another age. They marked our progress and gave us targets to reach or exceed. We took note of the stile numbers as we progressed; we had started at stile numbered 175, and finished at number 150 yesterday.

When we got back, we asked our neighbour if she'd enjoyed her late meal. Having had to wait so long, she'd lost her appetite by the time the food was ready to eat, and, to add insult to injury, it had given her slight indigestion. We sympathised with her. It was exactly the sort of setback that prevents a good day from ending perfectly. Our day had ended perfectly, however, and at night, the lighting on the refinery across the estuary provided a spectacular display, almost as good as a municipal fireworks show.

Our rest day had been good for us, despite the sunburn, and we got up for 7.30. Before we set off on our travels, we said goodbye to our neighbour. She marvelled at how so much stuff could be got into so little space, but she had her mobile home in which to transport her belongings, and had no idea what it was like to carry everything on ones back.

We were away by 9.50, and, shortly thereafter, climbing over our first stile of the day. There was a thin mist in the air; however, plenty could still be seen. We walked along to the accompaniment of the warning sound of the foghorn at St Anne's Head. As the coast swept around the bay, we saw three small tankers anchored in the centre, which became the focus of our attention for quite some time. We came to know the sight of them so well that we were able to recognise one of them, later in the day, when we saw it berthed in Milford Haven.

The grass had been cut along our route and this made walking easy. We came close to the first oil refinery to be built in this area. It was a strange sight, the small valley full pipes and valves but with no sign of life. There was a small beach with a large landing jetty, where we paused, like everyone else must do, and imagined what it was like before the refinery was constructed. However, as one guidebook points out, if we must have oil refineries, they have to be built somewhere. This one could have been worse, and the operators have made some pleasant concessions to members of the public who walk along the path.

Concrete steps led up from the beach. It was here that we were to leave the soft path and its rabbit holes behind and apart from seeing one more fort to match the one that seems to float in the middle of the estuary, our surroundings were very much man-made and modern; not that we minded modern things. After we had passed Gelliswick Bay and seen another large jetty, we trudged up the hill to Hubberston, where I had left the car. Our first stop was at the modern supermarket, which I'd previously discovered. We poked out our tongues at Milford Haven as we drove through, and, afterwards, we struggled to find the path again.

We gave up, eventually, and drove over the bridge to Pembroke and a lunch of kipper pâté, rusks and orangeade. We had eaten many lunches here in the past, and more were to come, not that we minded. It's a pleasant place in which to be, and we quite like eating, and it makes for a good combination. After a little more shopping for provisions, which included gas, we filled up four or five one-gallon water containers at Mullock Bridge, and went around Angle Peninsula, dropping them off at strategic places, with a view to camping there if all else failed. When I proposed that we make our way to Angle and the campsite, the girls welcomed the suggestion. We were all tired after what had been a very full day.

As usual, full advantage was taken of the showers, and Judith caught up on the laundry. The fees here were very reasonable, and we resolved to use Angle as a base.

Angle is a strange name for a place, and it is a strange place to describe. From where we viewed it, Angle Bay looks more like a lake than part of the sea, and the lake-like shallow slope down to its calm water makes it a good place for sailing small boats. However, when we saw it, there were very few yachts and no wind-surfers; it wasn't then a fashionable place. At that time, even the pub up at the point, which one passed on the way to the life-boat station, seemed to be twenty years behind the times, and the manager obviously made no effort to attract any of the jet set clientele.

The long main street, which is really the only one, is also the road to West Angle Bay. The walk from the campsite to West Angle Bay is not too long and is on the level. I had developed a deluxe blister on my heel, the first for years, a final testimony to the fact that I needed a new pair of boots, and a reminder that mountain boots are not always good for walking.

The site seemed reasonably quiet, although it was the height of the season, and we settled into the tent for a game of cards and a bottle of pop. I went out to the toilet after dark, and the sight of the Texaco refinery came as a big surprise. It was so brightly illuminated that it was like a miniature Manhattan, although it had more of a fairground enchantment about it.

Globe scale spectacular

Chapter 10

After some light rain showers in the night, the next day, a Saturday, turned out dry with some sunny patches. Before we left the site, I spoke to the farmer about the recent bad weather, which had spoilt his hay crop.

"I'd have done just as well if I had sat in the house for two days," he moaned. "You cut it one day, turn it the next, then you think, I'll turn it in the morning and get it in, but, of course, it rains."

As we were about to leave, I saw some girls getting in a tizzy with their small gas stove. They had tried to clip the new cartridge in, without unscrewing the top part and its piercing needle, and the cartridge was now half clipped in, pierced and spraying liquid gas all over her frozen hands. I'd had to fit many a gas tank, and it's a wonder there aren't more serious accidents, in view of the serious fire risk if it is not done properly.

We left at eleven; it would have been nice to think that we'd just put on our rucksacks and tramped away, but some more water caches had to be made. Next, we had to obtain some more cash and do some shopping at Pembroke Dock, which is a separate place from Pembroke. Afterwards, we parked our heavily laden vehicle in Monkton, ready for our next leg of the expedition. Before that, however, we enjoyed a salad lunch, potato-crisp sandwiches, apples and orange squash, which did much to restore our spirits and evoke enthusiasm for the task that lay ahead. This involved walking further along the road and down a lane, which soon became shady and afforded fine views of Pembroke estuary. After finding a slightly elusive stone stile, we found ourselves in a field that led us to a sewage farm. The next field contained a friendly horse, and he proceeded to follow us right through the field. The next stretch was on another lane, and it seemed hard to believe that this was the coast path. However, it was pleasant walking country, and certainly made for variety. It was as we were walking along this lane that my boots took another turn for the worse, and I noticed the sole was working loose at the front. A quick repair was effected by my passing the bootlace under the boot, and tucking it into the slightly modified tread, where it was my optimistic view that the lace wouldn't chafe through. In the meantime, Judith had found the spot where the path left the lane and led down to a small estuary overhung with trees. It was very quiet and matched my mental picture of Treasure Island.

From here, a series of cow tracks led us up a lane, which was narrow in the extreme. Even if the hedges had been trimmed, I doubt if two horses could pass each other there. It would certainly be interesting to know its history. About this time, we went through one of the many gaps in the hedge, to give ourselves room to remove our rucksacks, which is proof of how narrow it was. It was time for us to have a break and refresh ourselves with orange squash, rusks, mints, and peanuts coated with chocolate. We amused ourselves by trying to devise advertising jingles appropriate to our fare. This was typical of the nonsense conversations we had on trips like this, when the anxieties of life are not so much gone, but seen from a different viewpoint, life is taken less seriously than usual.

We continued to make our way down our very narrow lane as far as some woods, and, through the trees, I noticed a much overgrown fisherman's cottage. My imagination went to work instantly, and conjured up the imagined calls of children filling the woods, whilst their dad battled with the elements for their meagre living. It's strange how derelict houses conjure up in most people feelings of expectation, and a desire to see them live again, and know their past history, especially the little human details. All of which is probably behind the present craze for buying and refurbishing old houses.

As we climbed up the lane and out of this forgotten valley, we came to a farm and its attendant collie. He proved to be rather sly, and, with Joanna's fear of dogs, I wondered how we got past at all. Nonetheless, the gate was soon clamped shut behind us. We walked down a sheep pasture, towards the near silent power station, with its outlying pattern of roads and paths, one of which was ours, complete with tarmac, concrete steps and new stiles. This was a profound contrast to the general condition of the path on this section. This led us to the lane where we had left our water, and a little further on, we finished putting up the tents, just before it started to rain. Just before the rain began in earnest, a couple carrying large rucksacks walked up toward the Texaco car park. As the rain came down with increasing intensity, we wondered what their situation was, as we all huddled together in our tent, which was the slightly larger of the two. We were glad that we had remembered to proof the seams of the girls' tent, before bringing it on its first trip. I often hear of people who forget to do this, and give it no thought, until they hear the sickening drip of water, or see depressing puddles forming around them. Suddenly, we became aware that large puddles were surrounding us.

Our tents were on a small piece of stony waste ground, which had recently been levelled off while in a muddy condition. This was evident from the tyre marks and bulldozer teeth marks. It had since dried out into a lump as hard as concrete, making it almost impossible to get the pegs in through the many stones. Both tents stood side-by-side on the central island left by the tyre ruts. These, slowly and alarmingly, acted like a blocked gutter, as they relentlessly filled with water. In addition to this, as I went in and out, to fetch drinking water etc., the outer part of the tent became muddier and muddier, until we were left with nowhere to put anything down in the dry. Thankfully, once the water reached a certain level, it drained off into the surrounding marshy estuary. In spite of all of this, we managed to prepare and eat a good two-course meal, although there was an interruption that was due to an exhausted gas cartridge. This time, I remembered to pull the washer assembly down, before screwing in the new cartridge, and there was no wasted gas.

We even managed to wash ourselves in the tent. To make room for this activity, I went for a walk along the lane, which leads to a field bearing the romantic name of Texaco Car Park. The lane is steep and the view at the top was quite rewarding, as I looked down at the estuary and the jetties that now dominated the scene. The immediate scene behind was very much dominated by the refinery. Its size and complexity, coupled with our ignorance, produced in us a feeling of awe at the monstrous industrial giant that radiates across what used to be a quiet countryside.

That night, our camp reminded me of the Bible story of the Exodus from Egypt, when the Israelites were led by a pillar of fire by night and a column of smoke by day. We even heard the slight roar of the characteristic flame of gas on top of its tower. This flame was bright enough to cast shadows, even as far away as we were, and the surging brightness of its light could be seen inside the tent. We wondered whether the slight fumes emanating from the complex could have aggravated Joanne's sore throat, as she gargled, hoping that the process would frighten off any dreaded bugs. We slept very well, in spite of our huge, snoring neighbour, and awoke at 7.15, to find a soft rain falling; and it was Sunday, which, to many in the modern world, would mean a boring day. Ours was to be far from that.

It's an interesting topic – the fact that some things can be boring, especially to teenagers. The word has the same origin as bore, meaning to bore a hole, to make a void. If you paint a large area of concrete in a plain, light colour you also create a visual void. The normal reaction to something plain is to cover it with a pattern or pictures, which might be regarded as a civilised form of graffiti. This instinct to fill a void of space or time, when not satisfied, induces boredom. Simply to fill the void with something substantial is the logical answer, but it would be better still never to let the hole be formed in the first place. Nothing patches a hole as well as its original substance. To discuss what makes for a life of purpose and direction is well beyond the scope of this book. Nonetheless, our walks serve this purpose very adequately.

We managed to get packed in the dry, and were away by 11 o'clock, and soon crossing our first stile of the day, which was just past the Texaco car park. This was stile number 111, from the top of which you can see the estuary very well. The ships look more like mere boats, against the massive and yet spindly-looking jetties, which are, in themselves, quite a piece of engineering. One particularly interesting part of their design is the fuelling booms that carry tubes, which are attached to the ships, pumping the oil in or out. Their complexity is dictated by two factors. Firstly, they have to allow for the large tides of this area, while the ship is in dock, as well as the rise and fall of the ship itself as it is pumped full or emptied, whichever the case may be. With the very large, ocean-going tankers, known affectionately as a VLCC, this up and down movement can be as much as eighty feet. The acronym VLCC simply means Very Large Crude Carriers, these being ships over 200,000 tonnes deadweight. They are certainly vessels to be avoided by anything smaller, since a collision with one of them could have only one outcome.

Getting from this first stile down to the jetty was not too easy because we lost the path at one stage, although, when we did find it, lower down, the grass had recently been cut, the going was easy, and there was nothing to make our legs damp. Then, just after passing under the jetty, we sat by the quiet waters and had our lunch. From here, we had to pass along a short stretch where the ferns had received a council short back and sides. The cleared part came to an end just as we were passing a stray collie that just wanted to lie down quietly on the path. We had seen him wandering about, before we broke camp that morning, and could only speculate as to why he was there, seemingly well fed and in search of solitude. Collies are very sensitive dogs and can do some seemingly strange things, without humans knowing the motivating factor. I know a sheep farmer with a traditional black and tan Welsh collie that will play endlessly with the children and never bark. However, if he sees his master go through the gate, he's after him like a bullet, and, like most collies, when called upon to do so, he will work himself into the ground. Yet, when he comes back and sees the girls, he will find a piece of rubber, drop it at their feet, tilt his head on one side and appeal to their weaker nature. Yes, he's a very likeable and unusual dog. However, his master had had a particularly gruelling day, in the sheep pens, in the rain. He had never struck the dog, but, this day, under pressure, he had shouted at the animal. Later that day, the dog was nowhere in sight. The next day, he still could not be found. Eventually, he was seen wandering about on a nearby highway. Although his master joked about it, saying that the dog was trying to commit suicide, we were all amazed at the sensitivity of the dog, and how he had gone off with what seemed to be hurt feelings. Even if you don't like dogs, you'd have liked this one. I've since wondered if the black and white collie we saw that day had had a similar experience.

The path soon petered out and we got lost in a jungle of foliage, unable to trace the path at all. We reached a point where it was impossible to move any further, due to dense bracken and brambles. Then, as if by magic, Judith stepped over a low hedge, we followed and found ourselves back on one of those lost lanes. We enjoyed being able to walk along, virtually unhindered. The lane led down to Bullwell Bay, which, although dominated by the jetty, still retained an unspoiled air. The vegetation went right down to the sea. The sun came out and so did our lunch. While we sat there, the refinery put on a show for us, by bringing in a large tanker with about five tugboats in attendance. They turned the whole thing around and brought the monster in to berth, like ants bringing its helpless prey to their queen.

After a false start, we found the path off the beach, at our second attempt. Like stranded sailors, we worked our way into the interior, which was not too bad, after we had found our way into the comparative civilisation of a field, and, eventually, we came onto the road at Popton Point. Here, we came across another collection of buildings, belonging to yet another big oil business. There was also an old fortress, which the oil barons have landscaped and built their own castle around it. It is also interesting that no oil is actually refined here, but it is pumped underground to Swansea, and as well as that great feat of engineering, they also have a commercial pipeline from here to the Midlands.

The way from here follows the new road that sweeps around

the large Bay of Angle. We picked mushrooms on the grass verge, as we chose to walk here rather than on the bone-jarring, hard road surface. Walking along what seemed like a curved promenade, I could imagine it being crowded in the summer, and then, I realised it was high summer, in fact, it was Sunday the 28th July, and we had passed only one man, walking his dog. The new road turns inland after skirting about a third of the Bay, which has a substantial wall all along its length. Angle village, which seemed so near, when we were at Popton Point, now seemed further away, which, logically, we should expect it to be, after our long sweeping walk. However, from here, the path followed a very hard, stone-covered beach, and every jolt and tilt caught my blister.

At one stage, I viewed the length of the beach with despair and amazement, and wondered how such a small a wound could cause so much anguish. I was wishing that I had not left my flip-flops back in the car. We usually carried them, to wear as a comforting change at the end of the day, and they would certainly have been comforting right then. The tide was right in by now, and we could make no short cut, nor could we walk along the silt-type beach, which would be exposed at low water. The profusion of shells and dead crabs provided a pleasant diversion for the girls; however, the distant houses seemed no nearer, when we set off again. At last, we came to a little slipway belonging to a genteel estate, and this led to a private road, which represented the path into the village. Turning right at the pub sign, the road goes down to a causeway and over to the farm and camp-site where we had been, only two days before.

We erected our tents up at the top of a field, which was near a concrete road built for the tractor, and up and down this road went a little girl on a tricycle, breathlessly singing, "We're all going on a

Summer Holiday". In view of our tired state, we found the line "No more working for a week or two" amusing when we substituted the word 'walking' for 'working'. Our tiredness and hunger were soon dispelled by a meal of rice, corned beef and mixed vegetables, followed by bakestones and custard. Then, just as it had done yesterday, it started to rain, and it continued through the night, but now we had the convenience of the shower block, and so we all revelled in that, not knowing when the next opportunity to enjoy such luxury would come our way.

The next morning was Monday, and so, we were able to do some shopping in the village, before leaving just after quarter past eleven. On the road up to the public house were a few houses, and along came the occupant of one, who was on his way back from the beach, with a bucket-full of cockles. This made Joanna drool because she had acquired a taste for them when at Sandy Haven. Just past the pub, a gap in the hedge revealed steps down to the old lifeboat station with weather-worn foundations. A bit further on again and down on the beach, we nearly took the wrong path, which leads to the new lifeboat station. A family and their dog passed us, which reassured us of the prospects of a better path ahead. A girl also passed us, whom we recognised as a young mother we had seen with her family at the campsite, and who had obviously deserted them all, and gone off to enjoy some solitude, scenery and solace. At New Chapel Bay, Ruth began to complain of not feeling too well, and while we tried to dismiss the thought, we realised that this could well mean a failure to finish the path, this time around. Including the walk around to Freshwater East, the whole one hundred and eighty miles of Pembrokeshire's majestic coastline would have passed under our feet.

After a reassuring hug from us, our now not so little girl put her best foot forward as we moved ahead to the long awaited, dramatic, coastal change. As it came into sight, we saw again the Atlantic swell and felt the eternal wind in our faces, and we felt at home. Then, suddenly, after that teasing start, we were back down on the very homely beach of West Angle Bay. It was here that we made good use of its beach café, where we ordered seconds of just about everything on the menu. I watched Ruth wallowing in the warmth and comfort, and wondered how she would fare, as we still had a reasonable way to go. By way of encouragement, we bribed the girls with ice cream cornets and promises of an imminent return.

The path from here was only slightly overgrown, and once we had come up on the top, at East Block House, we had no trouble at all. A little later on, the situation had changed completely. Due to a profusion of wandering sheep, we had a profusion of wandering paths, but logic dictated the best course, and we continued to enjoy the now rugged coastal views. The views were equal in stature to the northern sections, near Newport. They were also equal in their ups and downs. Perhaps it would be more accurate to say downs and ups, and there were large fissures to negotiate, and also the attendant weariness. I had to carry Ruth's rucksack up the steep slopes and Joanna carried it on the flat. Ruth carried Joanna's lighter sack, when she could. Although the situation could have engendered feelings of anxiety, we all seemed quite able to cope together, which, as well as being pleasant, was also a great source of strength to us all, but particularly on this occasion to Ruth. We were able to enjoy the sighting of the many rabbits and sheep, as we sat down just past Sheep Island. It was with a very communal spirit that we discussed the things we had seen and were still seeing. We all commended Ruth for her obvious great effort, and she, being that bit older than her sister, felt guilty about holding us up. The toddler who had become a fine walker was fast becoming a young adult, but she still enjoyed a little nurse that afternoon, on those deserted cliff tops. Judith spoke with renewed enthusiasm about how grand it was to see the real sea again and also said how she would like to walk the whole thing again, but all in one go.

Joanna just seemed to be wallowing in the fact that she could carry Ruth's rucksack, and relishing the new delight of having a hip belt to take some of the weight off her shoulders. With the fresh taste of oranges in our mouths, we groaned ourselves upright and set off yet again. Then, the last few dips in the land before we reached Freshwater West really took their toll, and Ruth flopped down tearfully on the edge of the sand dunes. I had to carry her up to the others, and we decided that we would camp, here and now, among the dunes, because the next farm with camping facilities was a couple of miles up the road. So, while Ruth sat huddled up, with a pair of Karrimats wrapped around her, we hurriedly put up the tents.

It could be said that the peace and beauty of this place is not so much overpowering as under-powering; it lifts the spirit in a comfortable way. After seeing one last walker hurrying back in the opposite direction from that in which we had come, I made my way through a gap in the dunes, to see the mellow, red sky and the now shining and vibrant surf. The sea at Freshwater West is always exuberant to the point of being dangerous. The beach has quick sands and the sea has very strong currents, making it a very large beach, which is extremely beautiful to look at, and that was enough for that evening.

After we had finished our tea, someone came by and commented on the tents and how unusual they were, which I suppose they would be, to the average person. He was invited to have a closer look, and a pleasant conversation ensued. He was, in fact, the late walker whom I had spotted going back the way we had come, and he said he often came down after his work at the refinery. I reflected on the fact that, even down here, someone has to get away from the rat race. That led to him telling us how a dentist had come and camped down on the beach, some time ago. Seemingly, he had just left his job to come down here to live. After much persistence, the authorities managed to get him to move on. Our visitor reassured us that he thought we would be alright, and then went on to tell us, in a very knowledgeable way, about the tides and currents, with which he was familiar because his father was a retired coastguard. One point that I remember in particular is him saying how they had to sail the boat in an arc into the beach, when they crossed from headland to headland, so that they were not swept out to sea by the current. It was certainly awe-inspiring to think of such a volume of water, which has the weight of a mountain, moving about so rapidly. He also told us about his work at the refinery. To qualify for his type of work, like so many, requires graduate training, and then, to such an agile mind, the work becomes monotonous. There are many jobs like his, and hence the vast hoards seeking solitude in the mountains and along the edge of the sea. During the time we spoke, Ruth patiently lay in bed, with a temperature, and we were glad of the medical aids we had carried, although, in the past, I had grumbled at the resultant loss of precious space in our rucksacks.

Due to her fever, and her insistence that the outer door be left open, a sudden rain shower in the night meant that I had to nip out and close this door and drag our towels to safety. At 6.45am, we were aroused by the barking of dogs, when some people came to share their 'grand to be alive' feeling with us. Although we turned over and tried to get back to sleep, we also began to wonder whether we had been wise to have camped just here. Breakfast was a scene of serious discussion as to what was to be done for the best. Although Ruth was somewhat better for her rest, she was by no means fit for a heavy day's walking. We could have just gone onto the next farm and rested up for a couple of days, but we would then be low on gas, and so, it was decided that I should walk across to Pembroke and fetch the car, while Ruth rested in the tent. In spite of having had a good walk yesterday, Joanna insisted that she accompany me, and so, in pleasant sunshine, we set off.

Our first port of call was the WC in the car park, which I was very pleased to find open, firstly, for the obvious reason, and secondly, we were able to fill our water bottles and dilute our concentrated fruit juice. I had to be very careful at this point, to divert Joanna's gaze away from a notice, at which I kept looking in disbelief. Beware of Snakes! A quick trot up the road brought us to a small, thatched hut, which was built to store and dry a purple variety of seaweed. This is what is used to make the famous South Welsh delicacy called Laverbread.

Chapter 11

While we were walking down that country road and away from the sea, Joanna and I had a series of pleasant conversations, sometimes serious, sometimes silly. The baby had become an individual. This again emphasised the fact that everything is subject to changes. The deserted farms and their supporting land had been taken over by more successful neighbours, giving further evidence of changes in the farming industry. I had realised also that, since yesterday, changes had come about for us. It seemed that our Pembrokeshire backpacking was over, with the path incomplete. The final stages would have to be done as day walks, should Ruth get better in time, or as short trips, at a later date. There was to be no spectacular finishing line with attendant champagne and brass band. Nonetheless, in some ways, it was good that it had worked out like this, because that's how it is in real life; no Hollywood stories, just changes. On the way, we called in at Castlemartin post office and looked at the neat little stone village pound.

After an enjoyable meal of fish and chips, and I can recommend the fish in Pembroke, we drove back with yet more provisions to our remaining kinfolk. On our arrival in glorious sunshine, we saw that Ruth was up, one tent was down and most of the packing done. They told us what had happened. The local warden had come and asked if we had been there all night, and explained that we should not have been there and could well have been prosecuted. Judith had to explain how we came to be there and that I have gone to fetch the car. He had come back again a second time, and seemed to doubt Judith's story, and we were gone before he came yet again. We were grateful that he had been reasonable, and felt a little ashamed of ourselves, knowing we were in the wrong, and had quite rightly received a telling off. If you've seen Freshwater West Sands, you would appreciate how any form of abuse would ruin its natural beauty.

We then made off in an easterly direction, with the intention of making the other Freshwater a base, should we be able to walk the remaining section between the two Freshwaters, which was expected to prove to be the best part of this section. As soon as the tent was rolled out, more changes were to come. The shower stalls at the Angle campsite seemed more attractive, the sea was nearer, and the price would probably be lower. We packed up for a second time that day, with tiredness and tempers beginning to show. The hasty retreat was to Angle again, and the tent was soon up, with apologies all round. Once again we enjoyed the comforts of table and chairs, mattresses and other comforts, but I think they were enjoyed most of all by Ruth. We saw a girl lying sick in bed, in the caravanette across from our pitch, and could well sympathise with the family who lovingly cared for this seemingly uncomplaining patient. On the other side of us was something else altogether. We had to lie in bed and listen to a serious domestic dispute. It wasn't the usual verbal spat, but, sadly, there were the more serious whispered pleas, which they obviously did not want the children to hear. They appeared to be on the verge of deciding their future. Yes, we were back, not only among the crowded throng, but also back in the harsh modern society that witnesses yet further changes. The subtle, yet definite, erosion of the family unit was active, and so we treasured our affection for each other that bit more, and were grateful that our walking draws us closer together as a family.

We see how Dad's night out, Mum's night out, the kids at this club and that class, all lead to them rarely being together. We can appear to be isolated from each other, our eyes glued to the television screen, Play Station or computer. I suppose our family motto could be: Sharing is caring and caring is sharing.

We now embarked on a couple of lazy days, and Ruth was well enough for us to spend time on the beach and to take short, lazy walks. We strolled to West Angle, to watch the slow, colourful sunset, and it was really worthwhile. The evening tide was coming right up to the site gate, with hardly a ripple on the surface of the sea, due to the bay's extreme shelter. This was to the great delight

There were rumours

of all the boys on the site who had canoes, and we watched their antics until they began to run aground with the change of tide. In spite of our ice cream and barbecue kind of life, I was beginning to get itchy feet by the Friday morning. Judith would probably have put it the other way around and said I was like a pig with a sore head.

My desire to get the coast of Pembroke under our feet as a family and our being able to achieve goals that I had set for us all was not altogether the right attitude. At times of tight schedules, the joy of the passing path had been lost, and so, too, the joy of this last stretch was marred, not by Ruth's fever but my insatiable need not to be beaten. I well remember reading about the man who once held the record for climbing all the Welsh 'three thousand peaks'. Later in life, he regretted that his name should be associated with turning Snowdon into a race track.

And so our holiday took on a fitting end. The realities of life caused us to walk the last few stretches on day walks, as and when the MOD permitted us to do so. We were permitted to be there, despite World Wars and tank training, because we have legs to walk, because we have eyes to see. Permitted to do both because we have life and the things which support it.

The scenery on this last section is very photogenic and eminently suitable for day trips and day walks. Elygug Stacks and the Green Arch are bordering on being global-scale spectacular, and well worth the wait, should you arrive at a time when this section is closed. Saint Govan's Head appears to rule over many small and sequestered beaches. These include the much-visited Stackpole Quay and the very thought provoking St. Govan's Chapel. However, visiting Broad Haven and Barafundle Bay on a sunny day, or, as we say, a humming day, proved to be a high spot. Even now, we find that

Barafundle has made for itself a romantic niche in our minds, but perhaps that's a personal preference, and its magical charm could be gone, the next time we go. Nonetheless, all the scenery and the fascination of places such as the Lily Ponds seemed to lack that atmosphere which we had found whilst walking, that special thing that so few families have experienced. It's a form of communal solitude. Some sects try to turn it into an experience and expect it to provide contact with the inner self or the infinite deity, when basically it is just being at peace with oneself and the more than beautiful creation that God has given to us.

However, the end of our walk still seemed to be an anti-climax, and even whilst writing about it, there was that indefinite end. When I came to write down the story of our walks, it sat unfinished for a long time. All attempts at finding the finale left me at a loss for words.

I was talking to a site manager in work, one day. He was someone who was adamant that I finish the book, before somebody else put a similar book on the market. He died about a year later, and the crowd at his funeral was evidence of how many people knew and liked him. Crowds stood in the car park of his local church, which was packed full. He had done and said so much for so many, and was just a builder. He once told me of the time when his boys were young. He was worried about their getting into bad company and so he got them, along with their friends, to form a football team. Subsequently, he arranged with other teams of boys of the same age to have matches, until they were able to form a league. Then, as the players grew too old for their age group, he formed another team, and then another, and became increasingly involved in matches with other teams. One season, there was great excitement when their team reached the semi-final.

"Win this, boys, and we're in the final," he told them enthusiastically. As he told me the story, I could sense the affection he had for these lads, and could well imagine what they and their parents thought of him.

The players were on the bus, and on their way to this all-important match, with all the excitement and bravado of a fully professional team. Then one boy saw a young girl he knew and made some unsavoury remark.

"Stop the bus," my friend cried. The boy was told to get off the bus, which resulted in tears and pleas of, "I'm sorry, Mr Tew. I didn't mean it, Mr Tew." In fact, this potential league champion was reduced to a sobbing disaster. After what must have seemed a long pause and further pleas to Mr Tew, he was told he could stay on the bus, but the reserve would be playing instead of him.

In the changing rooms, the crisp, clean shirts were peeled off the pile as each lad came forward to collect his one. Every lad was rewarded with a pat on the shoulder from this gentle giant, who had led them so far. However, our shamed hero's number was not among those called, and the reserve eagerly waited to don his boots. No commendation was handed out to our shamed young man for last week's training, no gentle direction given to a potential genius. He merely received a piercing look from an oh-so-knowing eye. As tears began to form, a gentle voice asked, "Do you think you've learned a lesson?" When I heard that story, I had learnt one, along with many more.

It wasn't many months afterwards when this larger than life type man died. Whilst his death caused a great shock to me, and also many others, it also prompted memories of his many words of wisdom.

Many years later, the disciplined boy in the story, who had

walked down the street, saying respectfully, "Hello, Mr Tew", now walked along with a wife of his own. She would probably never know how much this Mr Tew had influenced the affection she received from the man in her life. It seems feasible to think that their marriage was partly held together by moral threads that were spun on that occasion, many years before, and both of them might be totally unaware of the fact.

So what about me, these many years later? How had I benefited from knowing Mr Tew?, I thought about how he pressed me to complete this glorified diary. My difficulty was in how I could complete it. Whereas before, our walk and this story had seemed unimportant outside the family, now things seemed a little different. I recalled his prompting, along with his great ability to recite words of wisdom, both at work and in the pub, and in verse or worse. However, there was one particularly memorable and borrowed recitation, which suited our situation.

"When the great scorer comes to call your name, it won't be how many goals you scored, but how you played the game."

The grand finale did not seem so important any more. There was tentative talk of the South West Coast Path. Now, there's an opportunity to ramble on even more, and, possibly, walk as well.

The story doesn't end quite here.

It was back to Sonny Terry and Brownie McGee and their inspiring song, 'Walk On'.

THE END (For now)

More books from y Lolfa

Welsh Valleys Humour

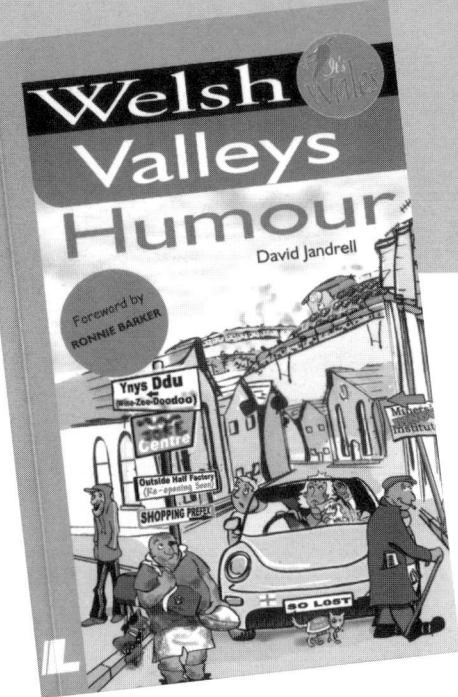

David Jandrell

A tongue-in-cheek guide to the curious ways in which Valleys inhabitants use English, together with anecdotes, jokes, stories depicting Valleys life and malapropisms from real-life Valleys situations!

£3.95
ISBN 0 86243 736 9

Rugby Trip Stories

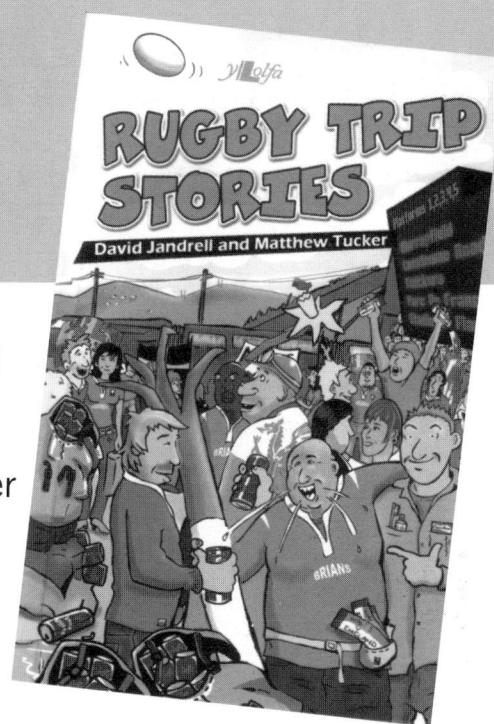

David Jandrell
and
Mathew Tucker

For the first time, the stories from the 'away trips' are published, for the wives to know what it's all about, and for the lads to read the funny things they can't remember...

£3.95
ISBN 0 86243 871 3

This book is just one of a whole range
of Welsh-interest publications from Y Lolfa.
For a full list of books currently in print,
send now for your free copy
of our new full colour catalogue.
Or simply surf into our website

www.ylolfa.com

for secure on-line ordering.

TALYBONT CEREDIGION CYMRU SY24 5AP
e-mail ylolfa@ylolfa.com
website www.ylolfa.com
phone (01970) 832 304
fax 832 782